DEFLATING
THE DARKNESS

Survivor Stories and a Prosecutor's Playbook
to Reclaim Power and Find Justice in
the Fight Against Sexual Assault
in Our Schools and Institutions

DEFEATING
THE DARKNESS

Survivor Stories and a Prosecutor's Playbook
to Reclaim Power and Find Justice in
the Fight Against Sexual Assault
in Our Schools and Institutions

HEATHER BROWN

Niche Pressworks
Indianapolis, IN

DEFEATING THE DARKNESS

Copyright © 2025 by Wayne Gross & Heather Brown

All rights reserved. No part of this book may be used or reproduced in any manner whatsoever without prior written consent of the author, except as provided by the United States of America copyright law.

For permission to reprint portions of this content or for bulk purchases, contact Publications@FightForSurvivors.com

Author Photograph by: Cristen Geller; GellerPhotography@gmail.com

Published by Niche Pressworks; NichePressworks.com
Indianapolis, IN

ISBN
Paperback: 978-1-962956-32-1
eBook: 978-1-962956-33-8

Library of Congress Control Number: 2025927738

This book is based on true events. It reflects the author's present recollections of experiences over time. The names, details, and characteristics of some individuals have been changed to respect their privacy. Some events have been compressed, and some dialogue has been recreated and or supplemented to maintain anonymity.

All materials have been prepared for general information purposes only, so as to permit you to learn more about the firm, services, and experience of the attorneys. The information presented is not legal or medical advice, is not to be acted on as such, may not be current, and is subject to change without notice.

Neither the publisher nor the author is engaged in rendering legal or other professional services through this book. If expert assistance is required, the services of professionals should be sought. The publisher and the author shall have neither liability nor responsibility to any person or entity with respect to any loss or damage caused directly or indirectly by the information in this publication.

The views expressed herein are solely those of Heather Brown and do not necessarily reflect the views of the publisher.

*To all of the survivors of sexual assault
who haven't yet unlocked their own superpowers:*

You deserve justice.

*Keep fighting for it, and don't give up.
Most of all, make your fight a light
in the darkness to help protect others —
because no one should have to suffer what you did.*

TABLE OF CONTENTS

FOREWORD	The Best of the Best	ix
DISCLAIMER		xi
CHAPTER 1	Facing the Darkness	1
CHAPTER 2	You Can Help Prevent Child Sexual Abuse	19
CHAPTER 3	How the Legal System Works	33
CHAPTER 4	The Silent Struggle	51
CHAPTER 5	The Process for Moving Forward	75
CHAPTER 6	Ready to Share Your Story? How to Prepare for Your Call	95
CHAPTER 7	Is It Worth It?	111
CHAPTER 8	Turning Pain into Purpose	125
CHAPTER 9	What Do You Need Most Right Now?	137
CHAPTER 10	Information for Parents and Teachers	145
ENDNOTES		153
ACKNOWLEDGEMENTS		155
ABOUT GREENBERG GROSS		159
ABOUT THE AUTHOR		161

FOREWORD

THE BEST OF THE BEST

Heather Brown is proof that it is not only possible to obtain justice for sexual abuse but to protect others from it too.

In this book, you're going to meet someone who can change your life. I know this because I've watched her transform the lives of countless others.

When I first met Heather, I knew she was the person to help lead the child sexual abuse litigation team at Greenberg Gross LLP. Not only is she a savvy, no-nonsense attorney, but she actually knows what the victims of sexual assault go through — because she has been there herself. Heather is a survivor of childhood sexual abuse, and her story is heartbreaking.

Despite that experience, Heather didn't allow herself to stay a victim. Instead, she chose to use her experience to help others who had suffered similar experiences. She has a long history of legal experience in key roles — as a prosecutor in the Orange County District Attorney's

Office, tirelessly advocating for victims and fighting for their rights; as a fierce trial warrior litigating numerous cases; and as a prosecutor in the Homicide Unit and in the Sexual Assault Unit (SAU), where for more than a decade she dedicated herself to prosecuting child molesters and rapists, bringing closure and justice to those who had suffered as she once did — in silence.

Throughout her career, she demonstrated not only grit and strength but an unwavering commitment to seeking truth and finding justice for victims. Her tireless efforts and dedication to her work have shaped her into a formidable force within the legal community, leaving an indelible mark on the pursuit of justice.

Heather's role as Special Counsel at Greenberg Gross LLP allows her to channel her passion and expertise into seeking justice against schools and organizations that cover up child sexual abuse. She provides a voice for the voiceless and a glimmer of hope for victims who once felt hopeless.

In *Defeating the Darkness*, Heather seeks to give you a path not only to justice for your own suffering but also to help prevent this kind of suffering for others as well. If you want healing, relief, and a way forward, you will find it in this book. As you learn more about how to take command of your situation and do something to help others, you can rest assured that others will be with you in this fight. You are most definitely not alone, and you don't have to figure it all out for yourself.

Whatever your journey forward, I wish you the best, and I know you will prevail against the darkness.

— **WAYNE GROSS,** Founding Partner
  Greenberg Gross LLP

DISCLAIMER

This publication is written directly to the survivors of child sexual abuse, which are often teens or young adults. It is intended to provide helpful and informative material on the subject matter addressed. Though the language is written for this audience, the author understands that a parent or guardian may also be reading it for or with the child.

Please note that some language may not be suitable for younger audiences. The material can include sensitive topics involving sexual and physical abuse, self-harm, substance abuse, and suicide, and can potentially cause triggering effects. Readers should consult their personal health professionals before adopting any suggestions in this book or drawing inferences from it. The author and publisher expressly disclaim responsibility for any adverse effects arising from the use or application of the information contained in this book.

CHAPTER 1

FACING THE DARKNESS

JASON: FROM VICTIM TO PROTECTOR

Thirteen-year-old Jason sat in the principal's office, waiting to learn his fate. His bruised eye throbbed, and his hands hurt from hitting the other kid. The fight hadn't gone on very long before a teacher broke it up, but it had taken its toll. Mostly on the other kid, Jason thought. He felt no satisfaction in that, only a dull emptiness.

Principal Wainwright called him in.

"Back again?" the principal said, tapping with his pen on a sheaf of papers stacked in front of him. He sat behind his huge oak desk, mounds of paperwork surrounding him.

Jason shrugged, slumping down in the old wooden chair across from the principal and kept his eyes downward, staring at his shoes.

"What's going on, Jason?" Principal Wainwright asked. "Last year, you were a model student. Now, all this year, it's been fight after fight. You're acting out in class, slipping on your grades, and becoming more and more withdrawn. Is there anything you want to talk about?" Jason heard the concern in his voice, but the last words hung in the air between them like an invisible wall.

Anything I want to talk about?

The question seemed so simple. Jason wished it really was.

No. I don't want to talk about it. I don't even know how to talk about it.

A lump formed in Jason's throat as he swallowed the words he wanted to say and went for the easier way out.

"Nope." He didn't look up as he said it.

It was better to be the bad kid than to tell Principal Wainwright the truth.

Principal Wainwright sighed. "All right; well, my door is always open if you want to talk. In the meantime, you have another week's detention. Next time, it'll be a suspension. I don't want to see you in here again like this, understood?"

"Yup," Jason replied.

"All right. You're dismissed. Get back to class."

For a moment, Jason hesitated, a part of him wanting to scream out the words that would change everything. *Why don't you know what's going on? Shouldn't you know? Why should I have to tell you?* And the worst question of all: *Would you even believe me if I did?*

Principal Wainwright, completely unaware of this turmoil, had already picked up his coffee and started to turn toward his computer. The moment was gone. Jason got up and left.

As he shuffled out of the office, mixed feelings coursed through him. Sure, he was glad he wasn't suspended, but he wondered what would happen if Principal Wainwright knew what was going on.

At this thought, Jason shook his head. The truth would sound ridiculous to Principal Wainwright. Heck, it even sounded ridiculous to Jason.

The worst part would be if Principal Wainwright thought it was his fault. Maybe it was. Jason's chest tightened.

Nope. It was better to just keep his mouth shut. Clenching his jaw in resolution, Jason walked a little faster, his secret still weighing in the pit of his stomach.

It would be years before he finally told anyone.

An Innocent-Seeming Friendship

Jason had grown up as the middle child with an older, more accomplished brother. Lacking confidence, Jason tried to find his way. Like his brother, he wanted to become a football star.

Jason's football coach, Mr. Maldonado, showed an interest in Jason.

"I believe you can become the star quarterback," the coach said. "I'll help you."

The attention was just what Jason needed. It gave him a ton of confidence. Jason's parents also appreciated Mr. Maldonado's interest in their son, and he became a friend of the family, spending more and more time with Jason.

They didn't just practice football, either. Mr. Maldonado also taught Jason to cook, bought him football cards, and let him hang out at Mr. Maldonado's apartment to watch the television shows his parents wouldn't let him watch.

Jason's parents were all too happy that he had a mentor. And Jason enjoyed the time they spent together. It made him feel special after being overshadowed by his older brother for so long.

What Jason and his parents didn't realize is that Mr. Maldonado had other intentions, and they weren't just to help Jason.

Unfortunately, this is exactly how perpetrators groom their victims. Buying gifts, special treatment, pumping up their ego, spending time with their family — all of this was designed for Mr. Maldonado to gain access and become a trusted friend.

Once he had gained the family's trust, things began to escalate. Mr. Maldonado found opportunities to touch Jason, giving excessive hugs, rubbing his legs after practice, or touching him a lot while talking. Eventually, the rubbing extended to his butt.

As their friendship grew, Mr. Maldonado began showing Jason pornographic movies and talking about sex. One day, Mr. Maldonado performed oral sex on Jason, telling him, "This is what men do."

Jason was embarrassed and confused. He was interested in girls, not boys; though, if he was being honest, physically it felt good at the time, which only added to the confusion.

Jason's parents also started asking him questions. One night, as they were cleaning up the dishes, his mom, Joanna, asked, "Is anything going on with Mr. Maldonado that makes you feel uncomfortable?"

"No," said Jason, feeling himself tense up as he ran the towel over the dish he was holding. It wasn't quite the truth, but he wasn't sure how to answer. A jumble of emotions and thoughts ran through him. He liked Mr. Maldonado. Was he uncomfortable? Maybe, but it also felt good. And Mr. Maldonado was his friend. He would feel guilty for telling on him — and besides, he had promised he wouldn't tell. He didn't want to break his promise.

"It's just ... he seems to be awfully attached to you," she went on, handing him another dish. "I don't understand why he gets so upset when you can't go hang out with him. It just doesn't seem normal."

"I swear, everything's fine."

He thought the matter was settled until later that evening when his parents came into his room.

"Your mother and I have talked about Mr. Maldonado, and we feel your friendship is inappropriate. We have asked him not to come to our house anymore, and we don't want you to go to his house, either."

Jason listened to this, the confused emotions still rolling around in his chest. He would miss his friend, but he was also relieved that the abuse would be over.

Unfortunately, things were far from over.

A Terrible Realization

Over the next nine months, Jason's guilt and shame mounted, and he became more and more isolated and withdrawn. He didn't know what to think about what had happened between him and Mr. Maldonado, nor what to do with all of his feelings.

He was acting out, and his grades kept dropping. He grew apart from his parents as they became more and more frustrated with his actions.

To make matters worse, kids at school were starting to discuss sex and whether they were virgins. Was Jason still a virgin? Did what happened make him gay? He didn't know. The confusion and shame spiraled. This formerly bright, cheery kid had now become angry at the world. His whole life had changed, and he didn't know how to deal with it. He felt totally alone.

Then, one day after school, Jason was sitting in detention, doodling in his notebook, when his football teammate Jessie walked in. Eyes cast down, Jessie slid into the seat next to Jason and proceeded to stare at the desk in front of him.

"Hey man," said Jason.

Jessie didn't move.

"Yo, earth to Jessie," tried Jason again.

Slowly, Jessie looked up and noticed Jason for the first time. "Oh, hey, man," said Jessie before returning his gaze to his desk.

"What are you in for?" asked Jason.

Jessie didn't look up. "Destroying school property."

"No kidding."

Yeah. I punched a wall. Put a hole right through it."

Jason whistled. He started to say something to Jessie again but stopped. Jessie had resumed his thousand-mile stare.

Jason's blood ran cold.

A memory flashed before his eyes of seeing Jessie get into Mr. Maldonado's car after a game to get a ride home.

And now, here he sat, another football player, eyes downcast, being punished for lashing out.

And in that moment, Jason knew Mr. Maldonado was doing the same things to Jessie that he had been doing to Jason. The nightmare wasn't over. It was still happening.

Jason wasn't the only one. He had to do something.

> *In that moment, Jason knew Mr. Maldonado was doing the same things to Jessie that he had been doing to Jason.*

That evening during dinner, Jason tried to gather the courage to tell his parents what had happened. He must've started and stopped a dozen times, but he couldn't quite say the words. Then dinner was over, and he had to get to his homework. He still hadn't said anything.

Finally, as he lay in bed at 11 pm that night, he couldn't take it anymore. He needed to turn his life around. He needed to save Jessie.

He got out of bed and went to his parents' room, where he found his mother in the bathroom, drying her face.

Joanna looked up. Seeing her son's serious expression, she set the towel down. "Jason, what is it?"

Jason forced the words around the lump in his throat. "I think ... I think Mr. Maldonado is abusing Jessie."

Joanna's face turned white. "Why do you think that?" she asked.

Tears began to stream down Jason's face. "Because he abused me."

Calling the Police

As he told his mother what had happened, Jason felt a terrible weight lift from his chest — one he had carried so long he'd gotten used to how heavy it was.

"I'm sorry, Mom. I'm sorry I lied for so long."

"Oh, honey. It wasn't your fault. I'm so proud of you for telling me." She put her arms around him, giving him a warm hug.

Finally, Jason pulled away, shaking, as fear welled up in him.

"But Mom — I'm not sure what Mr. Maldonado will do. He gets mad at every little thing. What if ... what if he finds out I said something and hurts our family?"

"Don't worry," she told him. "We'll call the police. They'll help us."

Jason told the police what happened (most of it, anyway; he still had trouble disclosing exactly how many times it had happened). They immediately wanted to gather hard evidence. They asked Jason if he would be willing to make a call to Mr. Maldonado to get him to confess while he was being recorded.

Jason still hesitated. Even though he knew what Mr. Maldonado did was wrong, he still felt like a tattletale. Mr. Maldonado had been nice to him. Didn't Jason get something out of this relationship, too? It felt wrong to turn him in because he had also benefited from it.

Jason looked at his mom. "What do you think?"

Joanna looked warmly at her son and reached across the table to grab his hand. She looked him in the eyes and said, "Let's nail him to the wall."

Suddenly, Jason thought again of Jessie. He thought about the hell he had gone through the past year. He thought of all the guilt and shame he was sick of feeling. And he thought about putting Mr. Maldonado behind bars to stop him from doing this to anyone else.

"Ok," said Jason. "I'll do it."

Getting Evidence

When Jason called Mr. Maldonado, he pretended he wanted a ride to purchase a birthday gift for a friend. The police were right there, listening to and recording every word.

After they talked for a few minutes, Jason started asking questions.

"Hey, why did you put your mouth on my penis?" Jason asked. "It made me really uncomfortable."

"I'm sorry," said Maldonado. He paused. "Are you alone right now?"

"Yeah."

"Okay. Did you tell anybody?"

"No. What would happen if I told?"

"Why are you asking that?"

"I don't know, I just —"

"Did someone tell you to call and ask me this?"

"No. This is just between you and me. I just need to know."

"Do you swear that you're by yourself right now?"

"Yes, I swear."

"Because if someone found out, I'd go to jail forever."

"It's just been bugging me."

Mr. Maldonado paused again.

"Look, I've had a lot of time to think, and I'm sorry for what I did. I screwed up. I've wanted to kill myself almost every day for what I did. I love you, Jason. You were like my little brother, and I screwed up."

"I just felt weird."

"I can't talk about this where I am at right now, okay? I'll talk to you more when I see you."

It didn't matter that Maldonado didn't want to talk about it anymore. The police had their evidence.

And then, the police brought his story to me. I would be the prosecutor on his case.

At first, he was still reluctant to talk about everything that had happened to him. However, when it came to protecting the other players on his team, he had enough courage for three people. We got to work trying to identify other potential victims, aside from Jessie. We looked at the football roster of all the players, and Jason told me which ones he had seen Mr. Maldonado pay special attention to or try to get alone. We gave the list to the police to investigate.

There's Never Just One Victim

We learned that Mr. Maldonado had abused more boys than just Jason and Jessie. There are never just one or two victims. In the end, four additional players disclosed being sexually abused and agreed to testify.

Jason was brave enough to come forward to start this chain of events, but he was still scared to testify himself. He was also worried that everyone at school would know what happened. And finally, he felt sorry for Mr. Maldonado. Jason felt responsible for getting him in trouble and knew this would ruin the coach's life.

And most of all, Jason feared that he wouldn't be believed.

For so long, he had denied that something was going on — he had even denied it to himself. He hadn't even told the police the full extent of what had happened. He didn't want to admit all the things that made him feel guilty or question his sexuality. He feared he would look like a liar.

As the prosecuting attorney, I was responsible for bringing criminal charges against Mr. Maldonado. Mr. Maldonado's defense attorney, meanwhile, would be trying to help him go free.

Therefore, I explained to Jason that he would have to tell the jury things he hadn't said before. And yes, the defense attorneys would do what they could to make Jason look like a liar because that was part of their defense.

"Every person I have worked with had the same fear that they wouldn't be believed," I said. "But you're not alone anymore. I have your back."

Jason thought back. "You know, I told my dad once that Mr. Maldonado was very huggy. My dad said, 'That's just how guys in sports are.' I think deep down I didn't say anything sooner because I felt like if my dad hadn't believed me on such a small thing, why would he have believed me about something even crazier? Why would anyone?"

Seeing the defeat on Jason's face, I said, "I believe you. And I know how you feel. I was sexually abused as a kid."

Jason looked up, surprised. "Really?"

"Yes. By my neighbor. And it was really confusing for me because I liked him. He was nice to me. I didn't have much of anything growing up, and he bought me presents and gave me attention. So, I didn't tell anyone for years. I felt so much guilt and shame about that."

"So, what helped?" asked Jason.

"This," I said. "Helping kids like you. I do this work to make sure what happened to me doesn't happen to anyone else. These perpetrators keep victimizing children unless someone stops them. Whether you know it or not, your speaking up is going to save many more kids, maybe even hundreds. Don't let what happened to you be for nothing. Your testimony is what will stop Mr. Maldonado once and for all."

Something shifted in Jason. And then he did something I hadn't ever seen him do: He smiled.

"Ok," he said. "I'm ready."

> *Whether you know it or not, your speaking up is going to save many more kids, maybe even hundreds.*

The Long-Awaited Court Case

Jason finally made it to the courtroom, where the jury listened to his testimony. Jason was the last of five victims to testify. He pushed through it, knowing it was for a good cause. After so many years of silence, he could finally speak out about what had happened to him.

As he stepped down from the witness stand, relief washed over him. It was palpable; we all felt it. He'd done his best and spoke the truth. Now it was time to wait for the verdicts.

A hush of apprehension fell over the courtroom as everyone waited for the jury to decide.

What would happen? Jason wondered, his whole body tense. Surely, there was enough evidence. Wasn't there?

Finally, the verdicts were announced. "Guilty, Guilty, Guilty. Guilty, Guilty."

Jason could hardly believe it. Mr. Maldonado was convicted of multiple counts of sexual assault and received a life sentence in prison.

Relief swept through the courtroom. Not only were the boys believed, but now this predator would never be able to do the same thing to any more boys. Jason and the other boys had done it: They had faced the darkness and won. Not just for themselves — but for others, too.

Transforming the Trauma

After this verdict, Jason would go on to thrive. Today, nearly 20 years later, he has a great relationship with his parents and is even in the process of taking over the family business. He's happily married and expecting his first child. He hopes to speak more about his story soon to help other survivors free themselves from the guilt and shame by having the courage to come forward.

He became not just a survivor but a protector. His courage enabled him to transform his terrible experience into a way to help others.

BETRAYAL OF TRUST: THE GROOMING FORMULA

One of the main sources of guilt survivors deal with is a feeling that they somehow betrayed the abuser's trust. In truth, it's actually the opposite situation. Perpetrators follow a specific formula to gain access to, target, and abuse children. **The formula consists of very specific behaviors to gain the trust of the child and/or the parents so they can perpetrate the abuse.** It looks like this:

Gain Access → Build Trust → Isolate → Share Secrets → Abuse

Gain Access: The perpetrator will get a job at a school, church, or recreational group. Then, they target vulnerable children or teens who are going through a crisis at home or who are children of single, overwhelmed parents with multiple children or jobs — anyone whose parents are less likely to notice strange behavior. Someone who has a solid home life is much less likely to be targeted, though they could be.

Build Trust: The perpetrator acts like a friend who just wants to help. In some cases, they may also befriend the child's parents or guardians. They are not worthy of trust, though they do everything they can to seem like a wonderful person. Their only reason is to get access to the child.

Isolate: Once they have trust, they find opportunities to be alone with the child. They may offer special lessons, extra coaching sessions, or much-needed babysitting. During these times, they knock down the kid's internal walls, acting "cool," telling jokes, or buying them gifts. They make the kid feel special, creating a "friendship." This bond is designed to make reporting emotionally difficult. The child will feel guilt and shame for betraying someone who trusted them with their secrets.

Secrets: Then, the perpetrator starts to teach the child to keep secrets. *Do you want to watch TV? Don't tell your mom. Do you want a beer? Don't tell your mom. Look at this porn. Don't tell your mom.* It often starts innocently enough and then keeps escalating. The child doesn't want the fun to stop, which means they are less likely to disclose abuse. It's also a way for the perpetrator to "get something" on the child. This instills fear, as the child will think that telling someone will get them in trouble for the other things.

Abuse: The perpetrator normalizes touching, such as lap sitting, hugging, tickling, wrestling, or rubbing cramps out of legs. When the perpetrator escalates this to sexual abuse, they'll talk about sexual things, like telling dirty jokes or showing porn. They might take pictures of the child posing naked or in their bathing suit.

All of this is specifically designed to confuse victims and make them feel guilty so they will keep quiet. That's why you should release yourself from the guilt and shame.

THE POWER OF SHARING YOUR STORY

If you are reading this book, I'm assuming that either you or a loved one has had a situation with child sexual abuse similar to Jason's experience.

The first thing I want to tell you is that it is not your fault. The horrible truth is this: Perpetrators like Mr. Maldonado groom their victims for the purpose of confusing them. Their actions are meant to put you at ease so they can gain your trust little by little before taking advantage of you. Just like Jason, you were a victim.

Do you have the same feelings of guilt, shame, and confusion that he did? Have you wondered whether people would believe you? Do you feel as if you didn't get any resolution or justice in your situation?

Did you report the abuse to police, but the perpetrator managed to get out of being sentenced harshly? Or maybe they got a light sentence or a slap on the wrist and went back to a new position, doing the same thing to others?

If the answer to any of those questions is "yes," then this book is for you. It is meant to help you take back your power by sharing your story. You can do something, not just to achieve justice but to help prevent this from happening to others, too.

WHAT THIS BOOK WILL HELP YOU DO

This book will help you go from being a survivor to being a protector. Sharing your story is just the first step. You also need to understand how to use the legal system to make a difference where it will count most.

You can't ever erase what happened to you or the effects you've dealt with throughout your life. However, what you can do is go after the institution that allowed the abuse to happen without setting any barriers in place to prevent it and without giving victims avenues for addressing it. Until organizations see that they have a responsibility to address these situations preventatively and immediately when they are revealed, the abuse will continue unchecked.

The U.S. court system allows for not only criminal cases but also civil lawsuits to be filed in cases such as this. For an institution to have a civil case filed against it can be devastating.

This kind of case isn't about just suing them for money (although that money has helped people whose lives were devastated because of what happened to them). This is about hitting negligent institutions where it hurts, in their wallet, thereby serving as a warning to other similar institutions. When a case like this is filed against one institution, the others all pay attention. They don't want the same thing to happen to them, and they will put their own guidelines in place to make sure it doesn't.

In this book, we'll explore several cases to help you understand your legal options for getting justice. You'll learn more about the system, get information for finding the right attorney, and know more about what to expect during the process. With this understanding, you're much more likely to resolve what happened to you and help prevent it from happening to others.

> *When a case like this is filed against one institution, the others all pay attention.*

WHY I CAN HELP

Remember when I told Jason that I knew how he felt because this also happened to me? Well, that's true. I know how you feel and what you're afraid of. I had all those same fears. I also know the power you have because I went on to become an attorney who specializes in these kinds of cases.

For years as a prosecutor, I put perpetrators behind bars, attacking the problem one person at a time through handling criminal cases.

Now, I am a civil litigator. Instead of filing criminal charges against the people who commit the abuse, my team helps victims file civil suits against the entire institution to ensure people like Mr. Maldonado are never hired and never have access to children.

I don't want anyone to have to suffer what you, Jason, and I suffered. I don't want this to happen to any more children. In my career, I have seen too much pain and wreckage. I have seen lives that have spun out of control — victims who can't hold a job or have a fulfilling marriage or who suffer from alcohol and drug addictions. Many go on to face a lifetime fear of intimacy and sometimes much more. Yet, I have also seen the light that comes from people who use their voices to stand up against evil. That sense of purpose can transform you.

What happened to you doesn't have to be your shame. I'm going to help you understand the legal process of a civil lawsuit, how it can help heal you, and how it can help to turn the tide on this epidemic. I want to put any fears you have about the legal process to rest and dispel all the myths. I want to give you the understanding and empowerment to join in this fight.

This is a global crisis, and if we want to do anything to effect real change, we all need to push for it. We need more people willing to use their voices. Together, we are powerful. Together, we can rise up against this epidemic and defeat the darkness.

CHAPTER 2

YOU CAN HELP PREVENT CHILD SEXUAL ABUSE

I'VE BEEN WHERE YOU ARE

Considering the kind of life I had growing up, I never would have thought I would be where I am today. I went from being just like the victims I work with — feeling traumatized, confused, and helpless — to being a fighter, the person who empowered them to stand up against evil and walk through the fire in order to protect countless others from being victimized.

My transformation wasn't easy. It took a lot for me to get here.

I spent my childhood witnessing and experiencing physical and emotional abuse at the hands of my philandering father. When I was five, my father divorced my mom and moved to Georgia to start a life with his new family. My mom moved us into a duplex in Dalton,

Massachusetts. It was a small, working-class town in the Berkshires, three hours west of Boston. This was the '70s and '80s, so picture lifted trucks, big hair, and small-town vibes all around.

To support my two brothers and me, our mom worked at a local radio station and tended bar. We were little hellions, the poor kids that everyone knew received free government lunches and who were often left to our own devices.

I really liked our neighbor and landlord, Mr. Warren, who lived in the other side of the duplex. He had a son my age named Johnny.

Mr. Warren was a lot of fun. Our basements were connected. When we would go through the door in our dark, dingy, scary basement to his basement, it was like entering kid heaven. He had games like Skee-Ball and pinball, a full working soda fountain, and an endless supply of chips, other snacks, and soda (which our mom said we weren't supposed to have). My two brothers and I were happy to play next door as we were bored and hungry for snacks after school — and hoping to forget our poor circumstances for a little while. We hung out over there a lot, along with the other neighborhood kids.

Mr. Warren didn't just have a great place for kids to hang out. He also gave me the time and attention I longed for from a father figure since my own father had abandoned us. Unfortunately, this turned out to be different from what I expected.

One day, when my brothers and Johnny were distracted playing pinball, Mr. Warren said we were out of orange soda and told me to get more from the kitchen fridge upstairs.

As I was looking around in the fridge, Mr. Warren walked up to me and grabbed my hand, telling me he wanted to show me something on TV.

He sat on his recliner, pulled me onto his lap, and turned on some cartoons. I was seven, and we didn't have a TV, so I was enthralled. Then, Mr. Warren started grabbing and fondling me, touching me everywhere. I froze, paralyzed by fear. He then moved me over to one side of his lap, unzipped his pants, pulled out his penis, and pushed my head into his lap, forcing me toward it. I was shocked, knowing this was not ok but not knowing what to do otherwise. It happened quickly, and soon, he pulled me up, zipped up his pants, and told me to bring the orange soda downstairs.

This wasn't the only time that happened, but that was the first time I remember. I tried to avoid Mr. Warren, but his house was so fun, and I still wanted to play with Johnny. There were quick moments of abuse and then more extensive ones when everyone was distracted. He was even so bold as to do this once while his wife was napping in the front room.

I'm not entirely sure why, at the age of seven, I consciously decided I would never tell anyone this secret. However, I do know that I liked Mr. Warren despite what he was doing to me when no one was looking. I liked his son, too. I thought, *If I tell, what's going to happen to Johnny? If Mr. Warren gets arrested, everyone will know it was me, and they'll treat me differently. We won't have a place to live, and it's going to be all my fault.*

I also thought I'd get in trouble for drinking soda (we weren't allowed to) if I told my mom about what he was doing to me.

I was a scrappy kid and thought I could just push it down inside me and keep it a secret forever.

Getting Away Brings New Trouble

We moved away from Mr. Warren when I was nine, and only because of a tragedy. My father went out hunting with a buddy and committed suicide by putting a gun in his mouth. After that, my mom wanted to give us a fresh start. She had been working multiple jobs, long hours, and tireless nights bartending to save up. She decided it was finally time to buy a house.

Needless to say, the situation with Mr. Warren, combined with my father's treatment of us and his tragic death, led me down a rough path. I was looking for love in all the wrong places and dating older men instead of boys my own age. I sought out the "bad boys," who I perceived as more fun.

When I was 16, I dated an older man named Eddie. He had been to prison, and unbeknownst to me, he was a drug user. I was so in over my head.

One night while he was on drugs, Eddie thought I was talking to another man and struck me across the face so hard I saw stars. I didn't call the police because it would violate his parole, and he would get sent back to prison. I was scared that when he got out, he would come and kill me.

Despite what I went through with him, I'm thankful because this experience shifted my perspective on the "bad boys." I realized they really are bad, and that nothing good can come from dating someone who doesn't value and respect women.

Hard Work and Miracles Pay Off

Fortunately, I happened to inherit my mother's intelligence (she would go back to college and get her degree in molecular biology). I decided I would go to Fisher College, a junior college in Boston, and become a travel agent. I had always wanted to travel, and my 18-year-old mentality thought this might be a good way to get inexpensive tickets to see the world.

The school conducted a math placement test and informed me and another student that we both had tested into Calculus II. The college also informed me they didn't offer calculus at their school, so they had hired a teacher to instruct just the two of us. One day, my professor kept me after class and asked, "What are you doing at this school? You're acing my calculus class. I've never seen you even crack open a book."

I looked down, embarrassed. "I can't afford the books, so I just didn't buy them."

"You're too smart to be here," she said, urging me to apply to a prestigious four-year university. I thanked her, not mentioning that I couldn't afford it.

Still, her comment got me thinking. A week later, I saw the Resident Assistant in my student housing building looking at a brochure for Loyola Marymount University in California. It was a school she had wanted to go to but couldn't get into. Loyola suggested she go to junior college first and then apply to transfer in.

She had an extra brochure, which she gave me.

A few days later, I pulled it out of my bag. As I paged through, admiring the beautiful campus photos and imagining what it would be like to attend, I suddenly thought, "Why not just apply?" I had nothing to lose. So I filled out the application and stuck the brochure in the mail, thinking nothing would probably come of it.

Little did I know how this small moment would change my life.

Two weeks later, my first miracle arrived. I was accepted.

When I called to tell my mom, she said, "I'll fill out the financial aid paperwork and see what happens. But we can't afford that, honey."

Then, the second miracle came. I had chosen math as my major on the application because I was good at it. It turned out that being a woman in math got me so many grants and scholarships that it was cheaper for me to go to Loyola Marymount than to my junior college! My mom helped me scrape the money together for my one-way flight to Los Angeles.

The campus was just as beautiful as the brochure promised, and I fell in love with it instantly. I worked a slew of odd jobs to make sure I could afford to stay — everything from on-campus work-study to nannying, even taking an elderly woman out weekly for dance lessons and fried chicken.

I found math boring, but my psychology class was fascinating. As I started learning more about the mind and how our environment can affect it, I thought more about my home situation. I also thought about Eddie.

I realized Eddie had gotten into trouble when he was young and ignorant, and after being incarcerated, his whole mental framework was shaped as a young man by the prison mentality. When he returned to live in a civilized society, he lacked the communication skills to get along with others in the real world.

I switched majors to psychology and decided I would become a parole officer. I wanted to try to help people like Eddie so they could change their lives and avoid becoming repeat offenders.

I started interning at the LA County Probation Office in their Narcotics Testing Unit. After watching parolees do the most outrageous things to avoid having their drug tests come back positive, I decided maybe I should help society by becoming an alcohol and drug counselor instead. Addiction seemed to be a terrible problem for so many — not just the addicts but also their loved ones and others affected by their choices. I started the certification process and got fairly far along when I suddenly realized what I truly wanted to do: I wanted to become a district attorney and put the bad guys in jail.

And so I began law school.

Miracle #3

It was during that time that a third miracle happened. While waiting tables at Nichols Restaurant in Marina del Rey, I got on friendly terms with a group of four men who always sat at the same table almost every day. One of them was in his 50s, and the other three were in their 30s. We always had fun, telling silly jokes and engaging in lighthearted chit-chat.

When I shared my plans to become an attorney, the man in his 50s whom I'll call Winston, was so impressed with my work ethic and the fact I didn't know he was incredibly wealthy and was nice to him anyway, that he hired me to help him with a legal battle. He needed help reviewing documents and compiling financial records for his legal team.

I worked diligently, uncovering countless lies and deception, and ultimately saved Winston millions of dollars in the lawsuit he was battling. He was so grateful that he kept me on the payroll and funded my entire law degree. We developed a Father Daughter relationship and he became the Father I never had. I thought I had hit the jackpot, but he would brush it off and jokingly say that my law school was cheaper than the attorney's fees he had to pay.

My Legal Career Begins

After finishing law school at Pepperdine Caruso School of Law in Malibu, California, I went on to take a job in the Orange County DA's office, where I got experience litigating cases. Eventually, I went on to a new role, trying cases in the Sexual Assault Unit.

This was where I felt I was finally doing what God intended for me to do. As a prosecutor and also a survivor myself, not only did I understand these victims, I knew how to help them. I could help them first find the courage to tell their stories. And then, I could help them win their criminal cases and put their abusers behind bars.

During my 10 years in the Sexual Assault Unit, I locked up hundreds of the most evil people on the planet. And yet, as I watched how the cases went, I began to realize there was a way I could have a greater impact: as a civil litigator, working to bring cases against the schools and other organizations that turn a blind eye, cover up, or fail to prevent childhood sexual abuse. Getting these institutions to change what they were doing and stop allowing this to go on would help protect everyone at these institutions.

During my 10 years in the Sexual Assault Unit, I locked up hundreds of the most evil people on the planet.

That was why I began working at Greenberg Gross LLP in their dedicated practice group, Fight for Survivors. My team focuses specifically on helping victims of childhood sexual assault by going after the institutions that turned a blind eye to what was happening to children under their care. Our goal is to get justice for our clients and help ensure the institutions never again fail to protect the children in their care.

Putting the Pieces Together

It wouldn't be until 25 years after my own abuse that I would learn how most molesters operate when targeting children — the Grooming Formula I shared in the previous chapter.

I learned how they create an environment to gain access to children, capitalize on the power differential, seek out the vulnerable ones, gain their trust, feed a need they have identified, and teach them to keep secrets so they will stay silent. It's this all too common pattern of grooming and typical reactions that ensures most children won't say anything if they're being abused — and it's how abuse keeps happening.

When I learned more about these things, I also realized that Mr. Warren rented specifically to my mom to prey on me. We were a broken family. My mom was busy working a lot. My brothers and I were playing in the predators lair. I was his prey and a perfect target.

DECIDING TO SPEAK OUT HELPS OTHERS, TOO

When I was abused, I didn't understand what had really happened to me and why my silence would create more problems. However, when I got older, I learned much more about how molesters operate.

One of the most horrible discoveries I made was what I've mentioned before — most perpetrators are repeat offenders. I thought that when we moved away, that was the end. I didn't get molested anymore. I didn't realize till later that after I got away, someone else took my place — or maybe they were already getting abused while I was. It was possible he was doing it to his son, Johnny, too.

The older I got, the more the weight of the guilt built up. The thought that it had probably happened to more children because I hadn't said anything made me feel worse than the actual abuse.

When I was 18, my mom called me and told me Mr. Warren had died. I started cussing him out like crazy. The wound had opened, and pure venom came out. I told my mom what had happened to me. She was rightfully angry and would have probably killed him if he

> *I didn't realize till later that after I got away, someone else took my place — or maybe they were already getting abused while I was.*

wasn't already dead (seriously). Meanwhile, I felt better and freer after finally just telling someone my deepest secret.

That's why I know it's my purpose in life to do everything in my power to prevent disgusting perpetrators from molesting children. I didn't do that with Mr. Warren, but I could do it now.

Within my caseload in the Sexual Assault Unit, all of the victims were age ten or under, or the perpetrator had multiple victims. With each new case, I would say to the child, "I want you to know this also happened to me, and I didn't tell anyone. I'm so proud of you for telling someone because you're my hero. I didn't have the courage, but you have the opportunity to stand up against evil. You're not alone. We're going to go through this together. Let's get this predator and save other children that this could happen to so that they don't have to feel the way you're feeling right now."

The more children we helped, the better I felt. The guilt went away altogether. I'm grateful I have the ability to relate to these victims and understand what they're going through. Oftentimes, when children realize their perpetrator is moving on to someone else, that's when they come forward (especially if the other person is someone they know and love). They want to be sure it doesn't happen to anyone else. I didn't get to do that with Mr. Warren, but it's what I get to do with these children — by helping to make sure their abuser is stopped in his or her tracks.

CHILD SEXUAL ABUSE IS AN EPIDEMIC

I want you to know you're not alone. About one in four girls and one in 13 boys in the United States experience childhood sexual abuse.[1] People known and trusted by the child or the child's family members represent 90 percent of child sexual abusers.[2] Overall, the prevalence of child sexual abuse is difficult to determine because it is often not reported; experts agree that the incidences are far greater than what is reported to authorities.

The majority of children do not disclose the abuse, with studies suggesting that only between 16 and 25 percent of children disclose the abuse to family and friends during childhood, and even fewer disclose it to authorities.[3] That leaves 75 percent of children being sexually abused without disclosing. The number of children being abused is astronomical and unacceptable.

> *People known and trusted by the child or the child's family members represent 90 percent of child sexual abusers.*

YOU SHOULD HAVE BEEN PROTECTED

Remember: What happened to you is not your fault. You were a child. You were carefully groomed by a predator who understood exactly how to manipulate you. The predator chose to work in that institution because that's where the children like you were.

This is the ugly truth: Molesters need access to children. That's why molesters are drawn to places like schools, aftercare programs, religious groups, and sports or scout programs — the places where we think our children are the safest.

The institution had the responsibility to protect you, and they failed. Maybe they didn't listen to danger signs, or they didn't pay enough attention to who they were hiring in the first place.

By holding the institutions accountable, we can be sure that the abuse doesn't happen again. Not by taking down one individual perpetrator but by forcing schools to be vigilant in ensuring no predators get in — period.

When institutions fail to protect children, we make sure to hit them where it hurts so it never happens again. We want them to ensure that when something's reported, they'll take it seriously and stop sweeping it under the rug. It's not about money. It's about how we save children.

YOU CAN DO SOMETHING NOW

You may have felt powerless after you were abused. However, you have the power to do something about it now, not just for your own healing but to prevent this from happening to more people. You can make a massive impact.

I urge you to speak up (or help someone you know to speak up) and join the fight or help someone you know. I know you're scared, but there's nothing more satisfying and healing than knowing you've protected a child. Oftentimes, our greatest struggles in life can result in our greatest strengths.

What happened to you doesn't define who you are. It's a bump in the road that you're going to have to get over, no

> *Oftentimes, our greatest struggles in life can result in our greatest strengths.*

matter how long ago it was. On the other side is empowerment and strength. It will give you a sense of purpose to take what happened to you and use it to change the world for the better. Standing up to evil is cathartic and healing, and it will transform you from a victim to a warrior.

CHAPTER 3

HOW THE LEGAL SYSTEM WORKS

MANDY, LEYLA, AND JULIE: STRENGTH IN NUMBERS

Mandy, a freshman, needed a new basketball jersey. The one she had been issued was too small. After school, she went to see her coach, Mr. Powell, to exchange it.

"You need a ride?" Mr. Powell asked when Mandy started to leave his office.

"No, that's okay," said Mandy. "I can catch the bus."

"Come on, I'll take you. It's on my way."

Mandy was grateful for the ride, which was much faster than taking the bus. And she liked Mr. Powell. He was warm and witty. The #1 song in 1979, *My Sharona*, was playing on the radio while Mr. Powell asked her questions.

"How are things at home?"

"Decent, although my mom and stepdad just had a baby, so I don't get much sleep."

"That's got to be rough, your mom starting a new family after all these years."

Mandy shrugged. She didn't want to say anything, but it was rough on her. She felt like she had been replaced. Her mother had previously been Mandy's best friend and biggest cheerleader, but now she had little time to attend Mandy's basketball games.

They pulled up to Mandy's house. Mr. Powell handed her a piece of paper. She saw it had his phone number on it. "I had a little brother who was favored his whole life, so I know what you're going through," he said. "If you ever need to talk, call me."

Mandy thanked him and went inside. She thought it was nice to have a coach and a teacher who really cared about her.

Over the next couple of months, Coach Powell offered her rides after almost every practice. She found herself lingering in the locker room to wait for him. Sometimes, they'd go through a drive-thru to get a bite before he dropped her off.

Mandy began trusting him, and before she knew it, she started telling him her innermost thoughts. He confided in her, too. His wife was just awful, and she went away on business so much that he only really saw her twice a month. She constantly pointed out everything that was wrong with him, and they argued all the time. They didn't even sleep in the same bed anymore. He was really unhappy, but she threatened to make sure he never got a dime if he divorced her. Mandy wondered how anyone could be so rotten to such a nice guy.

Mandy and Mr. Powell grew closer and closer, so much so that Mandy began to wonder if she was in love with him.

He started holding her hand in the car, and Mandy thought it felt really nice. It wasn't long before he began kissing her in the locker room after everyone had gone home. Then, it progressed to heavy petting.

Mandy didn't tell anyone what was going on for months. She felt like Mr. Powell was the only one in the world who understood her, and she wanted to keep him close. He told her it was too risky to keep making out at school, so he invited her to spend the night at his house while his wife was out of town.

What would she tell her parents? She decided to tell her friend Jenny so that Jenny would cover for her and say Mandy was sleeping over at her house. Jenny had her own secrets with older boyfriends that no one else knew about, so she knew she could trust her friend.

Mandy wrote a note to Jenny to tell her what was going on and to get her to cover for her on the weekend. She even wrote about her plan to give up her virginity to Mr. Powell. She passed the note to her in algebra class.

"Hand me that note!" their teacher, Ms. Edinger, said sharply.

Mandy's mind and heart started racing as she sheepishly handed over the note. *Holy shit. Holy shit. Please tell me this isn't happening. Mr. Powell is going to kill me. What if he loses his job because of me? Will we get in trouble with the law for being in a relationship? I'll just lie and say I was making a stupid joke.*

The bell rang.

"I'll drop you and this note off in the office now, Mandy," Ms. Edinger said. "Get your stuff. Let's go."

The minutes ticked by as Mandy waited for the principal to call her in. She hoped he would just throw the note away, and she would just get punished for note passing. After 20 minutes, Mandy heard someone call her name.

"Come on in, Mandy," said the guidance counselor, Mrs. Ramirez.

Perplexed, Mandy hesitated. "I think I'm waiting for the principal?"

"Nope, it's you and me."

Mandy sat down across from Mrs. Ramirez, who held up the note. "You want to tell me what this is about?"

"It's nothin'," Mandy quickly replied. She wanted to explain that it was just a joke, but the words wouldn't come out.

Mrs. Ramirez sighed. "Look, it's clear you have a crush on Mr. Powell, but he's married. I suggest you direct your teenage hormones toward someone your own age. I'm giving you detention for passing notes. If you get caught again, we'll have to call your parents."

Mandy was relieved. Detention she could handle. She would just have to be more careful in the future.

Mandy and Mr. Powell began having sex regularly at his home while his wife was out of town and even a couple of times in the locker room after practice. She thought she was special. She believed he loved her. She was 14. He was 38.

One day in science class, Mandy's teammate Tammy asked if she was going to the school dance with anyone. Things had been going so well with Mr. Powell, enough that Mandy decided to confide in her friend that she had a boyfriend, but that she couldn't take him because it was Mr. Powell.

"I thought he was dating Leyla," Tammy said.

Mandy's heart dropped into her stomach. "Where did you hear that?"

"She told me," said Tammy. "She's always going over to his house on weekends to have sex."

Mandy was heartbroken. How could this have happened? She wondered if maybe Leyla was lying to get attention. Then she saw Mr. Powell and Leyla together at practice and knew it was true.

Mandy was humiliated. She felt stupid for letting him use and manipulate her so easily. The depression she experienced only spiraled her further into self-destruction. She quit the basketball team, and her grades declined. She started smoking pot and having promiscuous sex. Once a bright young student with so much potential, she never went to college.

The Criminal Case

The following year, Leyla and another student Mr. Powell was having a "relationship" with would go on to report him. The school questioned him, and he denied it, so he continued to coach and teach. Instead, the school moved Leyla out of his class. She stopped playing basketball altogether.

Two years later, Mr. Powell moved on to Julie, a freshman who had just transferred from another school district. She was in the locker room one night after practice, and Mr. Powell pinned her up against the wall and kissed her while placing her hand on his

> *The school questioned him, and he denied it, so he continued to coach and teach.*

penis. She reported it right away to the school and authorities. Now, the school could no longer ignore the fact that they had a predator on their hands.

Mr. Powell was prosecuted but only got probation and a slap on the wrist in addition to being fired. The prosecution approached Leyla at that time to testify, but she felt guilty that she went along with the relationship and that it was her fault. She also felt like the school didn't believe her when she originally disclosed, so why would anyone believe her now?

None of these kids were thinking about civilly suing the school district for failing to protect them. They were in survival mode for years. Rumors had spread when Leyla first reported the abuse to the school, and she was treated unfairly and ostracized for making up "lies" against the beloved teacher and coach. Mandy never told her parents.

The Real Issue

Mrs. Ramirez's response to Mandy's note was a clear misstep on the school's part. They were officially on notice that something was going on but decided to chalk it up to teenage love and not deal with the bigger can of worms. There's something called *in loco parentis,* Latin for "in the place of a parent."[4] It's a common-law doctrine that basically means that during the time a child is in the charge of a person or organization (such as a daycare provider or a school), the person/organization has similar responsibilities to a parent's. Parents are counting on those individuals and organizations to look after their children and act in the best interests of their students.

Unfortunately, the school failed to do this for Mandy. They not only did absolutely nothing to protect her, but as mandatory reporters, they failed to do any type of investigation to look into whether they had a predator at their school.

Had that school counselor done her job and investigated what she read in the note instead of turning a blind eye, neither Mandy, Leyla, nor Julie would have had to suffer the sexual abuse they endured and the emotional toll it took on their lives thereafter.

AN OPPORTUNITY FOR JUSTICE

Many years later, at the age of 39, Mandy saw a television commercial advertising Assembly Bill 218. It took effect on January 1, 2020, opening a civil litigation window for sexual assault cases that had once been outside of the statute of limitations. AB 218 also increased the statute of limitations for sexual assault cases going forward.

Previously, childhood sexual abuse survivors in California had up until the age of 26 or within 3 years after discovering that sexual abuse caused their psychological illness or injury, to file a lawsuit.

Thankfully, AB 218 has increased the amount of time within which child sexual abuse victims can file a lawsuit. Under the new law, childhood sexual abuse survivors can bring civil claims until the age of 40 or within five years of their discovery of the abuse or that sexual abuse caused their psychological illness or injury.

The law also provided a three-year window for adult victims who were abused as minors to file civil sexual abuse lawsuits previously barred by the statute of limitations. That window closed on December 31, 2022.

Listening to the commercial, Mandy felt as if her bones had turned to ice. Was there still a chance to do something about her abuse?

All these years later, she couldn't shake the feeling that this major event in her teenage years had affected her entire life. She had been just a kid then, but the scars stayed with her. She had suffered through one bad relationship after another, and she still had issues trusting men, even after several years of therapy. She suspected her unpredictable bouts of anxiety and depression were also related to the abuse she had suffered.

Bolstering her courage, she decided to give our firm a call. She didn't want her fortieth birthday to pass without at least trying to do something.

Even though Mr. Powell was now dead, Mandy had a strong case against the school district, and the window was open for us to do something about it. When we started to gather information, we found a witness to help — Leyla. When we spoke to her, she asked us if she had a case as well.

She most definitely did. Leyla would never have been abused in the first place if the guidance counselor, a mandated reporter, had reported Mandy's note. So, we added Leyla to the lawsuit.

When we filed, we kept their names anonymous as Jane Doe 1 and Jane Doe 2. When a newspaper article about the story was published, a third victim, Julie, came forward, bringing our civil suit against the school district to three victims.

Once we went through exchanging information and holding the depositions of the three victims, the school settled the case for millions. In these kinds of cases, monetary settlement is based on the nature of the sexual conduct, the frequency, and the damage each survivor suffers as a result of the abuse.

After the mediation, Mandy asked if she could talk to Leyla and Julie. They accepted, and the women all met. They hadn't seen one another since high school.

They talked for two hours in a private room, bonding over their experience and sharing their compassion for one another. Mandy apologized to Leyla and Julie for not protecting them back then. They couldn't have known then as children what they know now as adults: They were preyed upon by a grown man who knew better. The only ones to blame were Mr. Powell and those in charge of protecting the students.

Aside from this cathartic, shared experience, Mandy, Leyla, and Julie now had extra money to help as well. No amount of money can take away the pain and suffering of survivors, but it does help them in multiple ways. It helps to recoup out-of-pocket expenses, such as medical treatment or therapy they've had to pay for over the years. It helps them get back some of the wages they potentially lost by not going to college due to this crime pushing them off their academic path. It helps them to heal in whatever way they need without the worry of financial constraints.

Mandy used the money she received to go back to school and finish her bachelor's degree. She now volunteers as a child abuse services advocate for at-risk youth, trying to be a source of inspiration and identifying youths needing extra attention in a healthy, uplifting way.

Leyla moved to Canada and bought a house with an art studio so she could paint. Julie used her money to get out of debt and help her daughter go to college.

In addition, the school was held responsible for their wrongdoing. The school district was forced to implement new policies on training, specifically outlining what staff, employees, or volunteers should do when they learn of students having "crushes" on their teachers. The school district was required through mediation to implement policy changes regarding coaches giving students rides home. Mandy might not have been able to save Leyla and Julie, but she certainly saved many more children.

This is just one example of how monetary settlement can bring about much-needed change.

When you've been molested, the biggest fear you have in coming forward — especially as a child — is that you won't be believed or that you somehow contributed to what happened.

Perhaps you went along with the abuse as a coping mechanism or plain survival. Perhaps you truly believed you had a special relationship with your abuser. These situations are all too common, as abusers often engage in a lengthy grooming process to gain their victim's trust (and ensure their silence). We have already seen how Mr. Maldonado did this with Jason and his family.

> *Mandy might not have been able to save Leyla and Julie, but she certainly saved many more children.*

THE CHALLENGE WITH CRIMINAL CASES

Unfortunately, with criminal cases, it is sometimes difficult to get justice.

The district attorney (DA) needs to be able to prove the charges, *beyond a reasonable doubt*, to 12 jurors. The legal definition of "beyond a reasonable doubt" is "an abiding conviction in the truth of the charges." *Abiding* means it sticks with you, and *conviction* means belief.

So, **the jurors have to believe that the charges are valid not just today but also in the future**; they must continue to believe it 10, 20, and 30 years from now.

Also, **all 12 jurors must be unanimous in their decision.** They ALL must believe that the defendant is the one who perpetrated the crime, that every element of the crime has been proven, and that there isn't any evidence that casts a reasonable doubt.

As you can see, a lot of pieces have to fall into place for a conviction.

A QUICK LESSON ON HOW THE U.S. COURTS WORK

Criminal cases are cases in which the government prosecutes an individual for a crime. **The district attorney (DA) or prosecutor** represents the government in bringing the criminal to court and helping ensure justice is served. Criminal punishment includes prison time, community service, etc. The person against whom charges are filed is called the **defendant.**

Civil cases, on the other hand, are non-criminal lawsuits handled by private attorneys. In these cases, a **civil litigator** serves as the attorney who helps bring the lawsuit against a defendant on behalf of the **injured party, or the "plaintiff."** The usual award the plaintiff seeks is known as **"damages,"** monetary awards to compensate for loss or injury due to the defendant's actions or negligence.

A **defense attorney** represents the defendant in either a criminal case or a civil lawsuit, working to protect the defendant's rights.

During the proceedings, a **judge**, the highest official in the court, will oversee the process, ensuring everyone follows the correct procedures. In jury trials, the judge acts as a neutral party to instruct the jury and offers instructions regarding the law. In criminal cases, the judge is also responsible for sentencing, or determining the punishment.

Additional terms:

Statute of limitations — the maximum length of time during which legal proceedings can be filed after the related event.

Witness — someone who knows something about a case and can testify to provide evidence.

The burden of proof — the requirement for a party in a legal case to show compelling evidence that what they are saying is factual. In a criminal case, the burden of proof is much higher than in a civil case, meaning the evidence must be much more compelling.

Therefore, the district attorney (DA) may decide not to prosecute the case if the prosecutor is concerned about whether the case is provable beyond a reasonable doubt, as described above. Sexual assault cases are especially hard to prove when the crimes happened many years ago, behind closed doors with no other witnesses.

The DA may also not be able to take the case because it falls after the length of time in which the prosecutor is allowed to file charges. Whether the crime happened or not, it is beyond the legally allowed amount of time within which criminal charges can be filed against the perpetrator. This timeframe is called the statute of limitations. It can differ from one state to another.

Even if the perpetrator is arrested, the DA for various reasons may have to negotiate a plea agreement and only put the molester behind bars for some small amount of time, which is not enough to punish them for the horrific crimes they have committed. And it will not protect future victims from suffering the same fate.

Any of these outcomes can have devastating effects on a child or the adult who reports the abuse later in life. To have the courage to speak out and then see that justice is not done feels terrible.

CIVIL CASES ARE DIFFERENT

Civil court cases differ from criminal court cases in many ways.

First, the burden of proof is much lower in civil court than in criminal court. Instead of requiring proof beyond a reasonable doubt, in civil court, the requirement is to prove your case by a preponderance of evidence. That means that it is more probable than not that the abuse occurred. It is more likely than not to have happened, based on the evidence.

Additionally, it doesn't require a unanimous decision. Only 9 of the 12 jurors have to agree that the plaintiff proved it was more probable than not that it happened.

> *The burden of proof is much lower in civil court than in criminal court.*

In fact, the real issue in civil cases is not about whether or not the abuse happened but is instead about whether there was knowledge of the abuse and thus an opportunity to prevent it, and what the damages are from the abuse being allowed to happen. This means that the attorneys must show evidence that the responsible parties within the school or organization knew or should have known about it and that the victim was physically and psychologically traumatized and damaged because of the sexual abuse.

WHAT THESE DIFFERENCES MEAN FOR YOU

Here's why pursuing a civil case is often a better solution than only relying on criminal charges:

- Criminal cases give you a chance to go after only the perpetrator, while civil cases allow you to go after the institution that failed to protect you.
- Criminal cases are meant to punish the perpetrator by putting them behind bars, while civil cases seek justice through monetary damages that also push

the institution to change the procedures or negligent activities that permitted the abuse to occur.
- Criminal cases are much more difficult to prove and win than civil cases due to the different requirements for burden of proof. Thus, you are far more likely to win a civil case.
- If you do win your civil case, you will make a much greater impact than with a criminal case because you will force institutions to stop practices that allow abusers access to children.
- Pursuing a civil case against an institution does not mean you have to pay your attorneys by the hour; the attorneys are paid only if you receive a monetary recovery for damages.
- And finally, a civil case is very unlikely to go to trial. Approximately ninety-five percent of civil cases are settled before a trial is needed.

CIVIL CASES RARELY REQUIRE A TRIAL

Many parents, family members, and survivors are afraid of going through a trial in which the survivor must withstand the jury's vigorous scrutiny and the defense's cross-examination. The truth is that trials rarely even happen in civil cases. **Approximately 95 percent of all civil claims are settled before a trial is necessary.**

For the 5 percent of cases that do go to trial, we are there to prepare you and make sure that you are protected, that your identity is protected, and that you are given an opportunity to use your voice to help create change.

Multiple Victims Matter

In a civil case, it's crucial to prove that the organization knew or should have known. This proof is difficult when there is just one victim. Unless there are some glaring red flags, such as the perpetrator is a convicted sex offender and the organization failed to run a background check, there's just one person saying it happened against others saying it didn't.

However, when you peel back the layers of the onion, there are usually other victims whose abuse the school either knew about or should have known about based on circumstances surrounding the events that led to it. These are things like the suspect having sleepovers with students, always "hanging out" with the students, giving rides to students or athletes, doing inappropriate things, making inappropriate comments, etc.

In the legal realm, when multiple people say the same things about the perpetrator, this is called "corroboration." Simply put, corroboration is other evidence that supports the claims of one party. The strongest corroboration is when two people who don't know one another are both stating the perpetrator sexually assaulted them. When there's another victim, it's not just a "he said, she said" situation where the jury has to decide which one to believe. It's two or more victims saying the same thing.

So, in short, the more victims who are willing to come forward, the more likely we are to win a civil suit, and it is easier in general to get justice with a civil case than a criminal case.

KNOW YOUR ASSEMBLY BILLS

New Assembly Bills are being passed in different states in regard to the statute of limitations for filing lawsuits regarding sexual assault. It's always a good idea to report abuse to law enforcement and reach out to a civil firm to analyze whether there is legislation allowing victims to seek justice. Here are the bills that have been passed in California (as of early 2024):

AB 218: Damages: Childhood Sexual Assault: Statute of Limitations

- **Expanded statute of limitations:** AB 218 increased the amount of time for victims to file civil lawsuits against abusers and/or entities that failed to prevent their abuse. Abuse victims can bring civil claims until the age of 40 or within five years of their discovery of the abuse and/or damages associated with their abuse, whichever is later.
- **Three-year revival window:** AB 218 created a three-year revival window for adult victims who were abused as minors to file civil sexual abuse lawsuits that were previously barred by the statute of limitations.

AB 2777: Sexual Abuse and Cover-Up Accountability Act

- Created for adult victims of sexual abuse.
- **Increased window**: Officially became law on January 1, 2023. The Act provides adult survivors of sexual assault a three-year window from January 1, 2023, through December 31, 2026, within which they can file a claim to recover any damages against an individual arising out of sexual assault crimes that occurred on or after January 1, 2009.

CHAPTER 4

THE SILENT STRUGGLE

When victims think about telling someone, a lot of different things can happen inside them to keep them silent.

Let's look at how some victims in two very different situations struggled with these inner conflicts and finally triumphed over them in the end.

ETHAN: OLD PAIN, NEW COURAGE

Ethan had never gotten over his guilt.

If I had said something sooner... would this have happened to others?

He was only thirteen when Mr. O'Conner had abused him. He'd been so confused. He had no idea how to handle a situation that felt so complex and overwhelming. And besides, he had always felt like it was his fault. If only he'd done something different... even the fact that Mr. O'Conner was arrested and put in prison never fully erased the guilt.

A Golden Opportunity

What happened to Ethan was very typical of the predatory Grooming Formula we saw in Chapter 1.

When he was 13, his parents were very active in their church and enrolled Ethan in the church's private school. The schooling cost quite a bit of money, but his parents felt it was important that Ethan and his two little sisters be in a safe environment with excellent teachers and curriculum.

One of their best friends, Mr. O'Conner, was also one of Ethan's teachers. Everyone thought he was the coolest guy. His whole mission was to help parents in the church cultivate their boys, teaching them to become men. He hung out with the dads, teaching them how to shoot guns and drive everything on four wheels. He stepped in where needed with single moms who had difficulties raising their sons on their own.

Ethan's parents had Mr. O'Conner over to their home regularly for Bible study and participated in many of the events he organized, including camping trips and church movie-night sleepovers.

One day, Mr. O'Conner suggested a great idea to Ethan's parents.

"I could really use some help with my pool-cleaning business," he said. "Do you think Ethan would be interested? It could help teach him the value of making an honest living."

Ethan was thrilled. Not only could he learn new skills, but he could also finally save up for that Xbox he'd been wanting, which his parents couldn't afford.

That summer, he and Mr. O'Conner began cleaning pools at big, fancy homes in Newport Beach and Laguna Beach. Ethan worked hard, and the cash started rolling in. He was elated as he finally got enough money to buy the Xbox.

Then, one day, Mr. O'Conner had him get into a pool to clean it. When he got out, Mr. O'Conner told him it was very important to wash off quickly and scrub with a special soap to get rid of the chlorine and chemicals that could damage his skin. He demonstrated to Ethan how to clean himself by putting soap on his own hands, and then started washing Ethan's body. Ethan felt strange about it, but told himself Mr. O'Conner was just looking out for his safety.

This pattern of washing off continued for a couple of weeks. Then one day, while leaving one of their affluent client's homes, Mr. O'Conner grabbed a note that had been left on his windshield.

"Wow," he said. "Look, Ethan, it's a note from the homeowner, Mrs. Devereaux. She used to be a sculptor in her younger days, and I heard she was pretty successful. She told me that since she retired, she only does a few sculptures now and then for art shows. Her note says she saw you cleaning her pool and was so impressed with your physique that she'd like to commission you to do a sculpture of your body for her upcoming art show! She says she'll pay you $300 for a few photos to use as inspiration. Wow!"

$300?! Ethan thought. *I could buy a bunch of games for my Xbox with that!*

Mr. O'Conner went on, still reading the note. "She says she needs the photos to be without any clothes on so she can make sure to do the sculpture right," he said.

Ethan was taken aback. "Um... naked? I don't think I want to do that."

Mr. O'Conner nodded. "I understand; that would be weird to have someone you don't know taking photos like that." They started packing up the equipment, and Ethan forgot about the note for a little while.

As they drove back to Ethan's house, Mr. O'Conner had an idea. "Hey, what if I took the photos?" he suggested. "I could crop your head out so no one would know it's you."

Ethan still hesitated. This didn't seem so bad... did it?

"There's no harm in that, right?" Mr. O'Conner went on, echoing his thoughts. "And besides, where else can you make 300 bucks in 20 minutes?"

Ethan couldn't argue with that, and he was already thinking about the game he wanted — and also another controller so his friend could play at the same time.

"Okay... but just promise not to tell my parents," Ethan said, feeling very nervous.

"Oh, don't worry," Mr. O'Conner replied, waving it off with a breezy smile. "It'll be our little secret."

The next day, while they were in the pool house at another client's home, they took the photos. Mr. O'Conner rubbed baby oil on Ethan, saying it would help him show off his physique. He also insisted the sculpture would look better if Ethan's penis was semi-erect and looked bigger.

Ethan felt weirder and weirder, but he'd already agreed to do the photos. When they were finished, he tried to forget about the whole thing. Mr. O'Conner paid him the cash the next day at work.

When he bought the games and the controller, he had mixed feelings. Making so much money like that seemed unreal and pretty awesome. It really hadn't been such a big deal, he told himself. His only worry was that someone would find out. And yet, how could they? And how would anyone know it was him, anyway? His face wasn't in the photos.

A few days later, Ethan was heading into school and heard a group of students whispering in the corner. As he got closer, he realized they were talking about a teacher who had been arrested.

"What teacher?" he asked, shocked.

"Mr. O'Conner," one of the students said. "They're saying he molested two kids. It's all over the papers." Ethan felt the horror course through him as he tried to process what they were saying.

And then the dread sank in.

The pictures. Oh, no.

He began sweating, his heart pounding. *What did I do? What did I allow him to do?*

Memories came rushing at him. The soap. Mr. O'Conner's excuses for touching him. He had known deep down it didn't feel right, yet he continued to let it happen.

He suddenly realized there probably wasn't a Mrs. Devereaux, either. Mr. O'Conner had just made her up as an excuse to touch his body and take naked photos for his personal use.

How could I have been so stupid? He thought. *And greedy!* He suddenly didn't care if he never played a game on the Xbox again. Over and over, he repeated these internal words to himself, beating himself up for not knowing better. He knew his parents would be furious with him if they found out what he'd done.

He resolved never to tell anyone, though worry still gnawed at him. What if those photos did have his face? Would he be arrested?

As emotions churned through him, he felt nauseated, and his head started pounding. He went to the office and told the nurse he wasn't feeling well, and she sent him home. He wanted to walk home and avoid his parents, but she made him wait. "You're sick. You shouldn't be walking anywhere."

Twenty minutes later, both parents picked him up. This wasn't normal. His heart began pounding as he saw their expressions. They knew. To his horror, they told him they wanted to talk to him about something important when they got home.

Oh my God, they found out about the pictures, he thought. He was in big trouble. The ten-minute car ride felt like hours, but they finally made it back to the house.

Sweating bullets, he sat down at the kitchen table with them.

"Ethan, we have some terrible news," his father told him. "Mr. O'Conner has been arrested." They explained the details he already knew. Then came a complete surprise.

"We know this must be hard for you, son," his dad said. "But we've got to ask you for your help."

Ethan was confused. Help?

"We know he would never do anything like this to anyone," his mother explained. "We were hoping you could talk to the kids at school and tell them to stop spreading rumors about him. And we want you to tell the police that he'd never do anything like this."

Ethan stared at his parents wide-eyed.

I can't believe it, he thought. *They believe him. I mean, why shouldn't they? He's their best friend. If I tell them the truth, it will crush them. They'll blame themselves, and they'll blame me. They'll think I'm stupid for believing this sculpture story.*

"Ethan?" said his father. "This is important."

They were looking at him with hope in their eyes.

Ethan wanted to be anywhere else right then. He hated to tell them something that would crush them. And yet, he couldn't lie. As hard as it would be to come clean, he thought of the other kids who had already spoken up without knowing it had happened to anyone else.

Finally, Ethan said, "I can't tell the police something that's not true." Their shocked expressions made him pause for a moment, but he pushed ahead, telling the whole story.

> *He hated to tell them something that would crush them. And yet, he couldn't lie.*

Relief and Justice

As he expected, they were furious. Except they weren't upset with Ethan.

They were furious with Mr. O'Conner.

They called the police, and Ethan told them his story, too. After Ethan, even more victims eventually came forward. At the trial, there were seven in total.

The jury heard from each of the seven boys who were victimized. Each told their story of how the perpetrator groomed them and convinced them to pose for naked pictures while finding opportunities to touch them sexually. None of the victims knew each other. This was very powerful evidence, and the jury found no reason not to believe each and every one of the boys.

The verdict came back after four hours of deliberation. At three counts for each victim, the clerk read "guilty" for all 21 counts. Mr. O'Conner was sentenced to 60 years to life in prison.

Though Ethan didn't know it, the story was not yet over.

It Could Have Been Avoided

Rebecca was the mom of a student who attended Ethan's school. It was a private school affiliated with their church. One Saturday evening, when the church held a Sunday school camp/Boys' Youth Group sleepover and movie night, she was happy to chaperone.

The auditorium was darkened as the movie played on the large screen up in front. Kids' sleeping bags littered the floor, and there was even a small table set up where the boys could get snacks, popcorn, and sodas.

After the movie, the boys finally got into their sleeping bags. She heard the typical giggling and goofing around as they tried to stay up as long as possible. She didn't mind; it wasn't too late yet.

Walking through the back of the darkened room, Rebecca saw a figure getting into a sleeping bag that was already occupied by someone else. She headed over to deal with the situation. As she got closer, she realized to her surprise that the person getting into the student's sleeping bag was none other than Mr. O'Conner, one of the school's most popular teachers. He was the one who had actually organized this movie night.

Suspicion prickling at the back of her neck, she hurried over faster to confront the teacher.

"What are you doing?" she asked.

Mr. O'Conner scrambled out of the sleeping bag, an embarrassed look on his face. "We were just joking around about trying to warm up. It's a little cold in here."

Rebecca's eyes narrowed. It wasn't that cold, and she didn't think he sounded sincere. "Why don't we turn up the heat, then?" she suggested. "Or you could put on a jacket. But you don't belong in a student's sleeping bag."

Still embarrassed, he quickly went over to the other side of the room, avoiding her after that. She kept an eagle eye on him the entire rest of the time, but he didn't do anything out of the ordinary. Still, he probably knew she was watching him, she thought.

The following Monday, Rebecca called the school and told the principal her concerns. His response surprised her as much as Mr. O'Conner's actions had.

"Now, we shouldn't overreact," the principal said, as if he felt the most important thing to do was to reassure her. "Mr. O'Conner is one of our most well-loved teachers. He's like a family member to many of the students. You wouldn't be upset if their father got into the sleeping bag with them, would you? I'm sure it's nothing to worry about."

Rebecca was furious. She couldn't do much else without the administration's cooperation, however, and she certainly didn't have enough proof of anything to bring in the police.

A few years later, when the boys came forward to bring criminal charges against Mr. O'Conner, Rebecca was the star witness, and we were able to put Mr. O'Conner behind bars.

Yet she never forgave the school administration for not listening to her. If they had, how many more students could have been protected from him?

A New Opportunity

Several years went by. One day, Rebecca saw a social media post that our law firm, Fight for Survivors, had just made about AB218, the new assembly bill that opened a window for old cases. She immediately contacted me to find out whether or not we could press a civil case.

"We need survivors to come forward again to pursue the case," I told her. "Otherwise, we can't do anything."

"I've been talking to the moms from before," she said. "We're working on getting their kids to come forward again." Their kids were now adults, and much time had gone by, so I wasn't sure what would happen.

I soon found out. With Rebecca's coordination, things began moving quickly. A few days later, I got a call from Ethan, who had testified at the criminal trial years before. He was now 23, a grownup. Prompted by Rebecca, his mom had talked to him about opening up the case to civil litigation to hold the school responsible.

"Do you really think this will make a difference?" he asked me.

"I do," I said. "What do you think would have happened if the school had listened to Rebecca?"

Ethan took a deep breath. "If they had listened, maybe what happened to me wouldn't have happened to more kids."

"Exactly," I said. "The only way to make them listen is for someone to take them to court and show them that what they did wasn't right."

> "If they had listened, maybe what happened to me wouldn't have happened to more kids."

He paused, and I could practically hear him thinking over the phone. After several long moments, he said, "Let's do it."

Released from Guilt

Ethan was only 13 when he was abused. Now, ten years later, Ethan and I found ourselves back in a deposition on the case, this time in civil court. This time, though, the timid 13-year-old had grown into a confident young man.

"Why didn't you sue the school then?" asked the defense attorney.

Ethan looked him right in the eye. "Because I was only 13 then. I'm 23 now. I'm not a scared and confused kid anymore, and now I know if the school had listened to Rebecca, maybe this wouldn't have happened to me and those other boys."

Ethan received a multi-million dollar settlement. Most importantly, in that moment, he went from being a survivor to becoming a hero and a warrior for others. He finally found peace with the guilt and pain he'd carried for so long.

MARIA, MARCO, AND DIANA: MANY VOICES BRING JUSTICE

I had a criminal case once with a little eight-year-old girl I'll call Maria, who had started wetting the bed when she never had before. (This is a common symptom of kids being abused.) Her parents were punishing her for it until she broke down and told them Juan, who was her babysitter Dolores's boyfriend, was making her do "bad things."

Maria's mom reported it to the police, which kicked off an investigation. Dolores assured the police that Juan had never been around the kids she babysat. They told her to stop babysitting at her house, and that was it. There was no case due to a lack of sufficient evidence and no corroboration.

Unfortunately, Dolores didn't obey them, and she continued her relationship with Juan.

Delores's son, Marco, was her child with her first husband, who happened to be Juan's brother. Marco was only ten at the time of the investigation into Juan and Maria.

Marco went on to have a rough life. He went to jail in his early 20s and became a heroin addict. His probation officer strongly encouraged him to go to therapy to help him understand why he was abusing heroin so he could kick the addiction.

In recovery, Marco disclosed that when he was five years old, his own father sodomized him. Marco had told Delores at the time, but she only hit him and told him to keep his mouth shut.

He had turned to drugs to numb the pain from what had happened.

Now in his late 20s, still living with Delores in a makeshift garage unit, he was clean and sober and had turned his life around. One day, he came home and walked into the kitchen to see Juan forcing a six-year-old girl to perform oral sex on him. Marco ran out, feeling nauseated and woozy, all his childhood memories slamming through him. He didn't know what to do.

He ended up telling the story to the one person he could trust: his probation officer. The probation officer looked Juan up and, sure enough, found Maria's report from ten years earlier.

"You have to be courageous," his probation officer said to him. "You have to tell the police about what you saw."

Marco was scared. Telling Delores what had happened to him had only brought him pain and a beating. Still, he knew he had to help now. He couldn't just turn away like his mother had. He went to the police and told them about Juan and the girl.

The little six-year-old girl, Diana, was scared of getting into trouble. When the police asked her if it happened, she said no. She was too afraid to tell the truth. Thankfully, later that night, she told her dad what really happened.

The Tie-Breaking Voice

This situation was complicated. We had a child who had now said two different things, and the only witness was a former drug addict with a checkered past. In these cases, we definitely need corroboration if we're going to have any chance of winning.

Enter Maria. Now 18 years old, she was very reluctant to come forward again. She didn't want to open the old wounds, and she was fuzzy on the details because she had pushed it all down.

The silver lining is that we had the videotape of her talking to the police right after it happened, when she was eight years old. The details were all there.

I said to her, "We need to stop this guy. We cannot let him get away with this again. It takes a lot of courage to even sit here and talk to me about it. If you hadn't come forward before, we might not have even had enough to nail this guy."

> *"If you hadn't come forward before, we might not have even had enough to nail this guy."*

"I don't want to," she said. Maria paused, closed her eyes, and took a deep breath. "But I will."

And she did. Along with her story, we had her videotape from when she was eight, and her mom testified about the bedwetting. We even found the retired police officer to come in and talk about her demeanor when he interviewed her.

Maria's testimony was the nail in the coffin for six-year-old Diana's case. Maria didn't get justice when she was eight, but her courage helped someone else years later. It also helped her with her own healing.

It was like a weight had been lifted off of Maria. A burden had come off Marco as well. He later told me that he was proud he spoke up because he felt like he had done something to break the cycle of abuse in his family.

SIX COMMON REASONS WHY VICTIMS STAY SILENT

The sad truth is that when these things happen, a lot of people don't tell anyone. They just want to move past it. People don't say anything for a variety of reasons. A few reasons come up often — and there are ways to fight through them.

As shown in the stories in this book, the following are common reasons people don't speak up.

1. "It's partly my fault."

Ethan felt stupid about what happened to him. He thought he should have known better. He was ashamed of how he'd been fooled.

This feeling happens to many victims, especially if they didn't speak up to stop the abuse. Throughout this book, you've read story after story in which shame plays a major role in not speaking up. Victims believe they are partly to blame for "allowing" it to happen to themselves or others, and they don't want to face that guilt.

This is a result of the calculated, premeditated grooming methods we've examined. These grooming methods are often designed to make you believe you were part of the decision so you will take part of the responsibility. You are supposed to feel ashamed and confused.

You were a child, and this person took advantage of the power dynamic between you and them. You were 100 percent a victim, even if you felt like maybe you participated or sometimes enjoyed the attention or even liked the perpetrator and now feel ashamed. That's why the predator grooms you — to complicate your feelings about yourself so you will be tangled up inside and remain silent.

"WHY DIDN'T I DO SOMETHING TO STOP IT?"

Victims often beat themselves up for "not doing something" at the time. If you've felt this, it's not fair to yourself. Here's why.

Maybe you've heard before about how, in threatening situations, people respond with the "fight or flight" response. This means they try to either fight or run away. Since you didn't try to fight or run away, you must have "allowed" it to happen.

However, did you know there's a third response? It's really a choice of "fight, fight, or **freeze**."

In all three of these responses, survival parts of our brain take charge to try to keep us alive and safe. Our brains try to choose the best response for the situation, so when we don't feel strong enough to fight or run away, we freeze.

Predators know this, and they take advantage of it.

We've already talked about how they carefully build trust and then take advantage of it to perpetrate their sexual abuse. They know that **children, especially, don't have the skills to defend themselves against the predator's methods and that children will freeze (I did) rather than try to fight or run.** The child will play possum, thinking, *Maybe if I stay still, he'll think I'm sleeping.* Or, *If I stay still, it won't be so bad.*

The predator expects these responses because he set up the situation to ensure the child will respond this way. It's not your fault.

These people are evil. And **you were the victim of that evil**, plain and simple.

2. "No one will believe me."

We've talked about this fear before, but let's look at it in more detail, especially in regard to the two stories in this chapter. When the predator is someone your parents trust or the cool teacher or someone at your church who everyone likes or respects, you can feel hopeless. "Who's going to believe me against them?" you think.

My whole team at Fight for Survivors will believe you. We believe you because we have seen this pattern of manipulation over and over again.

As we've already seen throughout this book, predators do things like befriending your parents and earning your trust to confuse you. As a child, you think that if your parents trust them, then what they are doing to you must be okay. Otherwise, your parents wouldn't be friends with them. It's the same thing with perpetrators who are teachers. The school trusts them, so why shouldn't you?

Knowing this makes it easier to see why you need to speak out, even if you're afraid no one will believe or listen to you. Marco even dealt with a situation in which he was silenced. If he had not been brave enough to speak out again, his voice would not have joined the others to win the case.

Sometimes, even though you disclose the abuse, it can seem like nothing happens, like what occurred with Maria. That can be frustrating. It's important to remember that perpetrators are repeat offenders. If there isn't enough evidence to convict them at the time, your disclosure could help someone else have their day in court down the road.

> *If there isn't enough evidence to convict them at the time, your disclosure could help someone else have their day in court down the road.*

In fact, thanks to Maria's courage in telling her story when she was still a child, precious details were recorded that may have been forgotten later. That recording eventually came around to take down the predator. Her bravery as a young child helped protect future children in a way she could never have foreseen.

3. "I'm fine. I can deal with this on my own. I don't need to tell anyone."

All of the victims in these stories had this feeling in some way or another. They thought they could just bury the pain deep down, and it would go away. They thought if they just didn't tell anyone, they could forget about it. However, that's not how trauma works.

If you're suffering in silence, your trauma will rear its ugly head at some point — in one way or another. Kept inside, it might be doing more damage than you realize. When trauma is left unresolved, our minds and our bodies use creative ways to try to resolve it themselves. These solutions can negatively affect your mental health, your relationships, and even your physical health.

Mental Health Ramifications of Trauma

The body keeps score, and what happens to it affects the mind. The crime might have "happened to" your body, but it's your mind that pays the price, and you can't escape it.

If you are robbed at a grocery store, you can get a new purse and go to a different grocery store. Over time, you forget about it. However, in sexual assault crimes, your body is the crime scene. You can't get out of it. The crime stays in your mind. I know this from my own experience and through talking with hundreds of survivors. The pattern is the same.

When you've experienced trauma, you have recurring thoughts about it. A tape plays over and over in your mind, pointing out all the things you could have done, should have done, and what you did to contribute to it. The guilt and shame can lead to emotional dysregulation, where you become numb and dissociate, or you act out and even have violent outbursts. It's believed that oftentimes, survivors will display these behaviors because they're trying to regain the control they lost when they were assaulted.[5] It's your brain's way of protecting you when things are too overwhelming, but it can become debilitating and lead to other problems.

Trauma often manifests in mental health issues such as anxiety, depression, obsessive-compulsive disorder, overeating, cutting, suicidal thoughts and attempts, and a whole host of other self-destructive behaviors. Marco's heroin addiction is just one example of this.

In sexual assault crimes, your body is the crime scene.

These coping mechanisms affect not just the individual but also communities and our entire society. When people can't cope, the collateral damage is astronomical. Hurt people hurt people. Substance abuse alone can ruin the lives of the substance abuser and their entire family as well.

Trauma's Impact on Relationships

Not surprisingly, these mental and emotional disorders also affect your ability to have healthy relationships. Mandy suffered from relationship issues over many years. As I mentioned, I had a poor relationship history until I dealt with my own trauma.

If you feel like you're unworthy or you're tainted goods — that nobody's going to love you because of what happened — that unresolved fear will definitely impact your ability to have healthy relationships. And your sense of unworthiness is just not true in any way, shape, or form.

I'm married to a lovely man, Tom Brown (a retired FBI agent), who adores me. I have three beautiful, smart, and loving children. When I told my husband about my abuse, he was nothing but compassionate toward me. It's been the same with everyone else I've told.

Trauma's Impact on Physical Health

Trauma trapped in the body can lead to physiological effects such as nervous system issues, heart and lung problems, digestive tract disturbances, and chronic pain. Studies show that people who experience unresolved trauma have higher rates of fibromyalgia and chronic pain. We tighten our muscles, which leads to stress, tension, and holding our breath. We can suffer from headaches, insomnia, heart disease, autoimmune disorders, and cancer.[6]

When we are able to talk about our traumas, we begin to release them.

To heal the mind and body, we have to experience the emotions that go along with our stories. Those emotions are locked away in our bodies. When we are able to talk about our traumas, we begin to release them.

4. "Will they come after me?"

There is also a fear of retaliation. Young people especially think, "If I tell, he'll come after me." Perpetrators often threaten children not to tell and instill a fear of something bad happening if they do.

In all my years as a prosecutor, I have never seen a perpetrator take any type of violent retaliatory action against a child or their family for coming forward. Not once. These are weak people who are always afraid of being caught and are always looking for ways to get out of things. Though they might call a child a liar or give a pathetic or ridiculous excuse, it is highly unlikely that they will physically go after anyone.

5. "I don't want to be known for this."

A lot of times, victims don't want people at school to know, especially if the perpetrator is a beloved educator. That was

Ethan's situation. Sometimes, it's parents who don't want to come forward because they're afraid everyone's going to know that this happened, and their child will be branded as a sexual assault victim.

No one has to know who the victim is. There are ways to protect your identity and keep you anonymous. Journalists are careful not to name the victims in sexual violence and abuse cases to protect survivors from worrying about what the public may think. Otherwise, they may not want to report the abuse or attack.

California Penal Code Section 293 (PC 293) allows a victim of sexual assault, domestic violence, or human trafficking to be referred to as "Jane" or "John Doe." This also applies to minors. It is very important that the attorneys request that a protective order be sealed per PC 293 as well[7] so no one can get the information from the court file.

6. "I don't want to get in trouble over this."

This goes along with the "being known" aspect. In this case, the victim is not thinking about what the perpetrator will do but what the people who find out will feel or do. The victim fears negative repercussions from others knowing.

For instance, Ethan was afraid to tell his parents because they were such good friends with Mr. O'Conner. He feared they would be angry with him for some reason. Little Diana was afraid she'd get in trouble, so she lied at first. Marco had already experienced his mother's anger firsthand when he told her. (Delores may have sided with the abuser because she feared the repercussions of doing something about it.) It's hard to go against the wishes of a parental figure or someone in authority, but Marco was willing to.

Diana's situation, in which she changed her story, happens often when children are suffering from trauma. Experts at our trials testify all the time about how one of the parts of child sexual abuse accommodation syndrome is recantation. A lot of children will say something and then take it back because saying it makes it real, and they don't know how to deal with it.

We also know that disclosure is a process. Sometimes, children test the waters. Psychologically, they may not have the ability to come forward right away. That doesn't mean they shouldn't be believed. Any jury on the planet will understand this means the child is suffering from trauma once it's explained to them by a trained professional.

Even if someone you tell doesn't listen, don't give up. There are people who will listen, who understand your hesitation and why you feel it is a big risk. If Maria and Marco had given up, Diana would have continued to be abused. And how many others would have, too?

THE RELIEF IS WORTH IT

Whatever fears you might have about coming forward, they are normal. It can be scary. That is your survival instinct trying to protect you further. The danger is over, and your mind just wants you to think it's not. And yet, everyone I know who has finally had the courage to tell their story has told me that they've only felt relief when they released it and said it out loud.

Even if you decide not to go forward with litigation, talking to a therapist about your trauma can be incredibly beneficial and therapeutic. The more you're able to get out everything inside you with a professional who can help you process it all and validate you, the more you'll understand that you're not alone and that you have support. You don't have to overcome this by yourself. There are people who really care and want to help you heal.

> *You don't have to overcome this by yourself.*

CHAPTER 5

THE PROCESS FOR MOVING FORWARD

Debbie didn't talk much. As she sat in our offices, I tried to catch her eye and smile to put her at ease, but she didn't look at anyone. For the entire first meeting, she pretty much gave one-word answers as she examined and picked at the ends of her hair. She didn't want to open up. She didn't even look like she wanted to be there.

We didn't blame her. Many victims have similar responses. Their lives have already been uprooted by what has happened to them, and going through the legal process means they have to expend time, effort, and emotional energy.

That's one reason we try to put all of our clients at ease and make everything they must do as easy as possible along the way.

I want to do that for you here, too, by giving you an idea of what will happen if you or your loved one decides to move forward with litigation.

Let's look at how Debbie's case proceeded to give you an example.

DEBBIE: BREAKING 30 YEARS OF SILENCE

Debbie had come to us wondering whether she even had a case.

In the 80s, when she was in high school, Debbie had dreams of going to Juilliard, majoring in drama, and becoming a professional actress. She was, therefore, thrilled when the school's drama coach hand-picked her as the lead for the school play.

He seemed very interested in helping her succeed in the role and invited her to his house to rehearse. He had her come back many times to "nail her lines," as he put it. After grooming her in textbook fashion, he raped her at his house one day. Debbie was devastated, but she also didn't want to lose her chance to shine as the lead, so she felt compelled to keep going back, enduring more rapes.

It turned out this "teacher" had a criminal history of sexual abuse and zero teaching credentials. The school hadn't run a background check.

Debbie had a really hard life as a result of that school's major mistake. She was nomadic, never staying in one place, never holding down a job for long, and didn't maintain relationships with any family or friends. She was haunted by this event her entire life.

Thirty years after the abuse, she reached out to ask us for help.

MOVING THROUGH LITIGATION: THE SHINE PROCESS

Make sure whatever law firm you plan to use has a clearly identified system that will take your mental and emotional state into account.

When a survivor comes to us for help, Fight for Survivors follows a process that takes the client through the proceedings one step at a time. We call this process SHINE, which stands for:

1. **S**hare Your Story
2. **H**old Them Accountable (by filing)
3. **I**nvestigate
4. **N**egotiate
5. **E**mpower

STEP 1: SHARE YOUR STORY

Making the decision to tell your story requires courage and determination. It might even be your first time disclosing to anyone. This is why we have a dedicated member of our intake team trained to help make this as easy as possible.

We understand this is a process that requires layers of trust, and this is just the first layer. You might be worried you won't be able to say much, as it's very common for victims to block out details from their abuse. We understand this. We know how to ask the right questions to help.

FINDING THE RIGHT WORDS MAY BE HARD AT FIRST

Talking about what happened to you may be difficult, especially if you've never told anyone before. It's all right at this point to speak in vague, general terms.

For example, "He sexually assaulted me," or "He made me do things I didn't want to," etc. You'll work through what happened, including the emotional impact on you, at your own pace. And we know how to ask the right questions to help you remember things you think you can't. Though it can be a slow process, it will be worth it.

The Intake Process

An initial phone intake is always the first step, where a member of our team collects your answers to basic questions — what happened, where, when, etc. — to see if there's a viable case. If we believe there is, we sign an agreement to work on contingency, which means we don't get paid unless the victim receives a settlement or wins at trial.

The first conversation is brief. You don't need to go into every single detail. If there is something you aren't able to talk about yet, you can speak in vague, general terms such as "he sexually assaulted/abused me." Sexual abuse can include kissing, touching, groping, oral sex, intercourse, masturbation, sodomy, or a mix of those things.

In the next chapter, we'll go into more specifics on what questions to expect, but here's a short list for now:

- Who did this to you?
- Where did they work?
- What was the nature of their employment at the school or institution?
- When did this happen?
- Were there any witnesses?
- Did you report this?
- Was anything done?

This isn't a call where we need the nitty-gritty details, but to get the information to see if we have a case.

After the intake call, you will speak to another team member who will do a more thorough intake, basically getting the whole story. This can be difficult, but we will help you work through the process. Our goal is to determine whether we have a case.

The Team Meeting

If we do have a case, the client then meets with our team to move things forward.

In that first meeting, we have our clients tell us a short version of their story. We will ask questions to make basic determinations about the lawsuit.

It's important to set expectations upfront. What do they want to happen in this case? What did the client set out to do when they called us?

We try to accomplish those goals for them, but the law only allows us to do certain things, and we want to make sure our clients understand the limitations. We can't always accomplish things like ensuring the principal is fired.

We let them know that there are no guarantees — there will certainly be disappointments along the way, and they could end up with nothing.

We also talk about what to expect in the process at a very high level, such as how long it might take to go to court, and we prepare the client for the next steps.

We usually tell clients that the first big thing they have to do is respond to written discovery, a kind of questionnaire with a lot of detailed questions. They have to look for evidence they might have, like old photos. They will have to tell their story about three to four times. I let them know there will be times when they will talk to me every single day for weeks, and then there will be months when they don't hear from me at all.

Most of all, though, in this meeting, we want our clients to feel comfortable, know exactly what to expect in this process, and realize they are in a safe space. We're going to be very close throughout this case and go through very personal details, so we always want them to feel like they know us and can talk to us. We want them to understand that we are 100 percent on their side, and we will do everything we can to not let them down.

We do this for them. We believe them. We have their backs.

STEP 2: HOLD THEM ACCOUNTABLE (BY FILING)

After our legal team determines that we can help you and that there is, in fact, a viable civil case within the time constraints of the law in which to file, we will then file a lawsuit (also known as a complaint).

The facts and details become even more important at this stage. Our legal team will draft the document, but we will review it with you for accuracy (either in person or via Zoom or phone call) before we file the paperwork to get the lawsuit going. This complaint is the legal document we use to put forth the basis for the lawsuit. We file it with the court and serve the perpetrator (if still alive) and the school or organization, as well as any other entity that was in a position of responsibility to keep the survivor safe from harm.

STAY THE COURSE

Keep in mind that the wheels of justice move very slowly. This is the natural process of litigation. There will be periods when we will need a lot of your help, as well as extended periods of quiet.

Fear not. Sometimes, a lot of work is going on between the attorneys, and we don't need the survivors to be a part of it. Sometimes it's procedural, where the other party is allowed sufficient time in which to respond to the filing. This is a part of our legal system, and it is unavoidable and beyond our control. The ultimate goal is to hold the institution accountable for its actions (or in-actions), so this often takes time, especially if the abuse happened years ago.

STEP 3: INVESTIGATE

In every civil case, there is a period in which both sides work up the case and prepare for the possibility of a trial down the road. This investigation phase is where we gather more details. For instance, if it was in a classroom setting, we're looking at the books assigned, information related to the teaching staff at the time, and anything small that might matter.

Witness Interviews

As part of the investigation, we round up and interview potential witnesses. This doesn't mean the sexual abuse must have been witnessed, as most sexual abuse happens in private. Witnesses can be people like the following:

- Friends you confided in about the abuse at the time
- Another teacher who warned you to stay away from the perpetrator's classroom after school
- A teacher in whom you confided about the abuse
- Another student who witnessed that you were clearly "the favorite" or were treated differently in the classroom
- Another student who witnessed the perpetrator always touching you or massaging your shoulders in class

Physical Evidence

We also look for actual physical evidence from the time the abuse was occurring, such as diary entries, yearbook photos, emails, or phone records. We'll look for records of any medical or mental health treatment sought after the abuse. None of this is because we don't believe you but because any and all of it could be important evidence to corroborate or substantiate the abuse in a court of law. The attorneys will be exchanging written discovery and, if applicable, have a survivor undergo medical exams or interviews with a psychologist.

Mental Exam

In most of these cases, there's also a mental exam with psychological experts, which includes psychological testing. This might sound like a lot, but clients often say it was easier than they thought.

Early Settlement Potential

School districts will often try to settle a case for fear of negative publicity or paying even more money for restitution down the road. Though rare, these settlements can occur at the early stages of the case. However, they generally happen after significant information is exchanged, such as through the depositions.

Depositions

In the event that the case doesn't settle early on, after both sides have exchanged information from their investigation, depositions are scheduled. This formal question-and-answer session is recorded and taken down by a court reporter, and it's when the full extent of what the survivor has had to endure is conveyed to the opposing counsel.

One of the hardest parts for the client is their deposition. We have to go through everything in detail, and it can be re-traumatizing and challenging to talk about feelings of guilt and shame. We know the idea of answering questions from another attorney and reliving what happened can be scary, which is why we thoroughly prepare you. You will not go into this alone.

We will be with you every step of the way and can object to something or ask for a break if the process becomes too overwhelming. Witnesses will have their depositions recorded as well. From these depositions, the attorneys on both sides get a feeling as to how things might play out in court should a trial occur down the road. Generally speaking, this is also where the monetary value of the case becomes clearer.

> *We will be with you every step of the way and can object to something or ask for a break if the process becomes too overwhelming.*

We do a lot of work to prepare the client for this so it doesn't feel so big and scary. While preparing for their deposition, clients can expect to meet with me or one of the other attorneys for hours, usually over several days. I let them know that the deposition can be antagonistic. However, most times, a good defense attorney is nicer because they are looking for facts versus treating it more like a cross-examination.

Oftentimes, as we prepare, I'll share similar stories of other survivors we've worked with (never revealing personal details) so they can see that they aren't alone. We share how we see the same patterns over and over again because we want them to understand that they did nothing wrong. They were truly victimized, and we don't judge them at all. I also want them to know that I have experience with these types of cases so they can feel confident in the team behind them.

We work a lot on how to talk and how to best articulate their feelings. It's a lot of asking questions and selecting the right words to use.

For example, I'll often ask, "How has this event affected your life?" This most certainly will come up in the deposition.

A common response is, "What do you mean? How has it not affected me? It's affected everything I've ever done in my life."

I have no doubt they are speaking their truth, but it doesn't reveal exactly how it's affecting them. Clients are often reluctant to share more because they are embarrassed about how it's affected them into adulthood, such as if they can't keep a job, have struggled with substance abuse, or have suffered failed marriages. So, I ask more questions. How has it affected your personal relationships? Do you have a relationship with your mother or father? Do you have a relationship with your husband/your wife/your children, and how is it?

We have a lot of male clients who share how they struggle to bathe and change their children, feeling as though they don't know the proper boundaries. I had another client who could never hug his children because he didn't understand the proper physical boundaries. "I've never been able to hug my child" is more compelling than "It's affected my whole life."

Remember, we are preparing our clients for the legal system. A client's story is their story, and they should feel free to share it however they want with whomever they want. However, when it comes to the law, we need to be able to explain it in a way that will give them the best outcome.

STEP 4: NEGOTIATE

It is costly for anyone to pay for litigation through a trial, and sometimes, the benefits of a settlement outweigh the risks associated with litigation.

Settlement

Sometimes, school districts or organizations will offer a settlement before a lawsuit even gets filed. This is done by way of a demand letter, in which our team drafts our intent to file a lawsuit. The institution then may make an offer to settle (though this happens less frequently).

More often, the opposing side wants to see the strength of the civil case against them before negotiating a settlement. After evidence is gathered through the investigation and the deposition process, parties sometimes opt to engage in mediation. In such cases, a neutral third party, often a retired judge, acts as an intermediary between the parties and encourages them to reach a settlement. However, if a settlement is not reached, the case can proceed to trial.

Our team will advise you if we believe a settlement is in your best interest, but ultimately, the power and choice of going forward with a jury trial or settling is 100 percent your decision.

Trial

Trials are often the hardest part, with the defense counsel trying to pull the victim's story apart. They can last about two weeks before the jury comes back with a verdict. However, we always let our clients know the statistic I shared earlier: Approximately 95 percent of all civil cases — whether they are sexual assaults, breach of contract, or car accidents — settle before trial. So, in all likelihood, a settlement will happen.

Approximately 95 percent of all civil cases — whether they are sexual assaults, breach of contract, or car accidents — settle before trial.

STEP 5: EMPOWER

Whether you choose to go forward with a trial or settle your case, you may receive monetary compensation for your abuse. It is through this accountability and "hitting them where it hurts" (in their pocketbook) that things will begin to change. You will also have a sense of purpose, knowing you stood up against evil and that your voice had the power to hold institutions accountable for failing to protect you. You will have been a part of that change.

Unless and until we rise up and let our voices be heard, the abuse will continue. Schools, organizations, and institutions will continue to get away with failing our children. Taking action can't erase the abuse, but working to obtain justice and bring about necessary change can certainly help restore your peace.

Afterward: A New Perspective Brings Peace

While every client acknowledges that the process is difficult, most experience a feeling of empowerment and the weight of guilt and shame lifting. Often, this is the first time they were able to disclose what happened to them, and they find strength in their story.

They've opened the door to speaking about it, so they are more comfortable in sharing. After feeling powerless, many clients feel they were able to take their power back because they finally sought accountability for what happened to them.

DEBBIE'S CASE

Debbie did fine on her initial call, which was very brief and gathered only basic information. Then she moved to the next step, in which another team member did the more thorough intake questions, basically getting more of the story.

This was tough for Debbie. One of the questions we asked was for details about her schooling. She said, "I can't remember."

"Can you please try?" asked my colleague. "We really need this. We're obligated to provide this information in the case."

Debbie was flustered. It was so long ago. "I really can't remember," she said.

"I understand," my colleague replied. "There is so much required information in a case that it can start to feel almost invasive and controlling. A lot of survivors feel that when they are required to do things for the case, it's like a personal attack. And that's not our intent at all."

Debbie wasn't reassured. Later, she confessed she was thinking, *I'm the one that was abused. Why am I the one that has to do everything?*

My colleague explained that, unfortunately, the people seeking justice have the burden of proof, so we have to prove the case, and to do so, we need to answer certain questions.

Debbie worked through this part, giving us the benefit of the doubt.

When the full team met with her, we could tell right away that she was smart, no-nonsense, and very matter-of-fact. We told her that her trial might take two to three years, which is pretty typical. None of this goes quickly, which often ends up bothering clients more than they think it will.

Debbie's case was no different in that respect. At first, she hated getting on the phone with us and often wouldn't pick up or call back. When we could get her to talk, she was often angry that we weren't further along in the litigation.

As we got to know each other better, things went more smoothly. Instead of our having to struggle to get her on the phone, Debbie started calling us frequently for updates and opened up more. She started to trust us, and that transformed our relationship with her.

We never judged her for her initial reluctance to cooperate. It's important to understand that everyone in Debbie's life had let her down. For Debbie, nothing anyone did was ever good or right enough because nothing in her life had ever been good or right. Trust didn't come easy for her. The system had failed her, as it has with every victim we work with. It took a while for her to see that maybe this time, things could be different.

As we kept going through the process, she started to recognize that we were her allies. We were there to make a difference for people just like her. And we understood how she felt.

As we prepared Debbie for her deposition, we asked her questions like, "What other teachers were around?"

At first, she answered, "No one was ever around."

A little later, as she thought more about her situation, her response became more compelling. "I was a kid," she said. "I wasn't keeping track of all the people that were supposed to be looking after me."

When it came time for her to be questioned by the defense, the opposing counsel asked her why she was filing a civil lawsuit. I'll never forget her answer.

"He got a slap on the wrist compared to my lifetime of misery."

In the end, Debbie decided not to go to trial and received a multi-million dollar settlement. Payments typically take

60-90 days, so we often tell clients to wait to make big life decisions until the money is in hand.

"What will you do now?" I asked her on the phone on the day after the settlement came through.

"I — I'm not sure," she said. "I think I want to go to school. I don't know what major yet. And I want to buy a house and settle down in one place. It would be good to have some stability in my life."

I was thrilled. She was finally starting to feel more at ease and move on from her trauma.

Debbie ended up quitting her job and renting a place for a year before deciding where she ultimately wanted to settle down. The settlement gave her the freedom to live anywhere, to start over.

DO I HAVE A CASE? THE PATTERN OF NEGLIGENCE

All too often, we hear stories about how a young student had the courage to report abuse to either a trusted teacher, guidance counselor, or even a parent. Unfortunately, instead of being met with compassion and shared outrage, those in authority actually re-victimize the victim.

This is one of the ways we're able to prove negligence. We'll often see that the principal or other school officials said the student must have "misinterpreted conduct" or suggest the student might have a motive for lying.

We've had cases where the head of the institution tried to get the victim and the perpetrator in a room together to "talk things out" without involving anyone else (such as law enforcement). This is a clear effort to mitigate damages on behalf of the institution, not the victim. There is nothing that can be worked out because there is no excuse for an adult to inappropriately touch a student.

Another "solution" we see is when the school puts the perpetrator on a short administrative leave, only to have them return with no notice to the victim. Now, the student has to be in the same room with someone who not only harmed them but who is also aware that this particular student reported their inappropriate behavior to the school.

Their grades suffer. They might stop going to school and have to retake classes (impacting graduation). They have to worry about a re-offense and feel incredibly alone and vulnerable because they feel like they have no one on their side (or that no one believes them). This situation emboldens the perpetrator to re-offend because the environment allows for it.

The school may then try to minimize interaction, which only makes it more challenging for the student. They'll tell the student they can just sit in the hall during class, or they give the student extra bathroom passes for any time they feel uncomfortable and need to leave. This is not a solution. It requires the student to approach the offender for permission to leave and can also spark uncomfortable rumors amongst other kids. The school may suggest that the student switch classes, but the only option might be to a lower level or to a credit they don't need. It sets the tone that it's on the student to do something about the problem when it should be the other way around.

I had one case where a teacher was terminated and criminally prosecuted, which was appropriate; however, the student was so psychologically traumatized that she attended counseling on a regular basis just so she could continue attending her school. The school threatened that because she had missed so many classes, she wasn't going to be allowed to graduate. The only reason she was missing school was that she could barely get out of bed in the morning due to the school's negligence in hiring a predator.

School districts and other institutions have a responsibility to their students, first and foremost. They have to learn to vet their teachers vigorously. They must also supervise, train, and monitor their staff. Staff should be trained to identify potential dangers and signs of abuse. If one perpetrator slips through the cracks, they must take every measure to fully investigate and ensure the victim and perpetrator have no further interaction. The institution must do so without further costing the victim or making it their responsibility. Civil cases that hold these institutions accountable will help to change these patterns that we see all too often.

School districts and other institutions have a responsibility to their students, first and foremost.

CHAPTER 6

READY TO SHARE YOUR STORY? HOW TO PREPARE FOR YOUR CALL

The thought of calling a complete stranger and telling them your story to see if you have a case can be anxiety-provoking, at the very least. What will you have to say? What are they going to ask? What kinds of things could happen?

We recently fielded a call from a young man who was sexually abused by a doctor. He was terrified to open up about his abuse, playing down what he thought might have happened for fear he would ruin this doctor's reputation.

Unbeknownst to this victim, the "good doctor" actually had 27 other known victims. When we told him this, he was relieved to finally know that he wasn't imagining anything; he really had been abused. He was scared when he first picked up the phone, but once he went through the process, he was happy and relieved he had made the call.

If you're contemplating a civil lawsuit but feeling overwhelmed about the idea of disclosing, you can start to prepare by documenting each element of your story. So that there are no surprises, write down the answers to the following intake questions, which you can expect a law firm to ask you.

1. Who did this to you?

The reason this is the first question (and is so important) is that every law firm handles different types of cases. It would be disheartening for you to tell someone your story during an intake call (maybe even for the first time) and be told, "We don't handle those types of cases," so it's best to know in advance who can actually help you.

At Fight for Survivors, we only handle cases where a school or institution is involved. This could be a high school, elementary school, employer, college, church, sports, organization, medical facility, or extracurricular group. You might have a criminal or civil case for sexual abuse, such as familial abuse, but we do not handle those cases. Many other lawyers out there can help with familial cases.

We specialize in civil cases against institutions because we believe this is the way we can help prevent childhood sexual assault on a large scale. We also want to help you receive a settlement, and when you go after individuals, the cost of litigation is often too high a risk. However, institutions often have insurance to be able to pay survivors if the institution appears culpable, or guilty of negligence.

2. What was the perpetrator's role?

We want to know if the perpetrator was a teacher, coach, or other hired employee or volunteer. We need to establish that they were in a position of trust and that the school or institution was responsible for the conduct of that person. This means the institution had a responsibility to vet or properly supervise this person.

3. Where did they work?

If there is a viable lawsuit, the attorneys need to know the organization that will ultimately be named in the lawsuit. There might be more than one party to be named. For example, if the perpetrator was a doctor at a hospital, the doctor and the hospital may both be sued. This is also important because if a case moves forward, the law firm will need to research assets to see if the institution or professionals had insurance at the time of the abuse.

4. What did they do to you?

Depending on the extent and frequency of the abuse, the answer to this question will help the attorneys gauge whether the pursuit of a lawsuit will ultimately be advantageous to you financially. Basically, these facts will play a role in the amount of monetary compensation your case will warrant. Your answer also helps us to understand the depth and breadth of the abuse so we can refer you to get proper support from others as well (such as a therapist who specializes in your particular circumstance).

5. When did this occur?

This is key because it will let the attorneys know if your case is within the statute of limitations (the time in which we have to file a lawsuit). This is often a complicated analysis, as many new assembly bills are continually being passed that allow past sexual assaults to be civilly litigated. These assembly bills often include "lookback windows" that provide a period of one to three years in which the law allows us to file a lawsuit for crimes that happened long ago and may otherwise be outside of the statute of limitations.

Additionally, new laws regarding sexual assault are continually being passed as the legislature acknowledges that survivors don't think about a lawsuit right after an assault. Victims often operate in survival mode for many years before being able to even think about taking this step. (For the latest assembly bills in California at the time of this writing, refer back to Chapter 3.)

> *New laws regarding sexual assault are continually being passed as the legislature acknowledges that survivors don't think about a lawsuit right after an assault.*

6. Who did you tell (if anyone)?

Survivors have the right to file a civil suit, even if they never reported or told anyone about the abuse when it happened. They can bring a civil lawsuit regardless of whether criminal charges were pressed. However, in order for us to file a civil lawsuit, we must be able to prove that the school or institution, or your employer had "notice" somehow that their employee was a predator or was engaging in questionable behavior.

What is notice? Notice can be called "actual notice" where the survivor actually told the school. It can be something called "constructive notice," where the institution had knowledge that the perpetrator was doing something inappropriate or was reported to have done something inappropriate. Or it can be a "constructive notice" where they should have known or had reason to suspect.

For example, constructive notice would apply if there were rumors that a teacher was getting cozy with the students after school or if the perpetrator had a prior conviction in another state for sexual abuse. There is liability on the part of the school district in cases of negligent supervision as well, such as allowing the teacher to have sleepovers at their home. Were there any red flags that should have alerted the school that something was wrong and put them on notice?

Many scenarios can be construed as notice. It basically boils down to a "they knew or should have known" standard. Certainly, if the survivor told another teacher who is a mandated reporter and this teacher did not notify the school, we can prove notice. We once had a case where a student had written a class essay in which she wrote in detail about her relationship with another teacher, how she was in love with him, and planned to have his baby. That is arguably notice, and the teacher she wrote the essay for should have reported this immediately.

Finally, this question also provides information on potential witnesses and can help assist with proving the survivor's case.

7. Was it reported to a person of authority?

Is there a record of it being reported to anyone? A school nurse, school counselor, another teacher, the principal, or anyone in a position of authority? If the abuse was reported to the school or institution and they did nothing about it, that is considered notice.

On the other hand, if it was reported to someone other than the school, such as a therapist or physician, the report could provide corroboration of the abuse and provide a paper trail documenting the details of when the abuse occurred (and help locate additional witnesses). This reporting could also help prove that the school should have known about the inappropriate behavior.

If the case was reported to the authorities, such as campus police or the local police, there would be police reports and investigations that we would want to obtain for the civil suit. More importantly, these investigations often contain key witnesses as well as potential other victims.

8. What, if anything, did the institution do in response?

If the school or institution was notified and did nothing, they are negligent in their handling of the report of abuse. If, after the institution was notified, the perpetrator was not fully investigated and was placed back into their position (where they could potentially sexually abuse more children), this could also be the basis of civil liability.

Moreover, by not taking appropriate measures, the school or institution further victimized the survivor. The victim may have felt as though they were not believed or that they were punished for reporting.

All of these situations can show that the institution did not protect the students, and those facts can be factored into the civil case for the amount of damages.

9. How has this impacted your life?

Damages typically equate to the amount of money that your case is worth in the eyes of a judge or jury. We're assessing the impact to gauge the damage to your life because of this event. In general, the more severe the damages, the more your case is worth.

There are many different ways sexual assault can affect a survivor's life. These include physical harm to their body (like diseases or pregnancies), mental problems such as insomnia or anxiety, addictive behaviors, or circumstantial problems such as trouble with relationships, trust issues, or the inability to hold a job. All of these negative outcomes happen at a cost to you. Assessing damages helps to put a number on the effect the event had on your life.

10. Were they ever criminally prosecuted?

Not only do police reports contain valuable information about the abuse, but they often contain information about other victims the survivor may or may not be aware of and could potentially lead to witnesses and/

or corroboration. Sometimes, a criminal case contains admissions and confessions that can be useful in a civil case. A criminal conviction for the underlying abuse proves that it occurred in the eyes of the law, which is incredibly helpful for the civil case.

Even if the criminal case didn't end in a conviction, this does not mean that a civil case cannot be filed. The burden of proof in a criminal case is much higher; it needs to be proven beyond a reasonable doubt to 12 jurors. In civil cases, the burden of proof is a preponderance of the evidence, which means (more likely than not) that the abuse happened, and the school or institution was on notice and either was negligent in hiring this person or failed to properly supervise.

INTAKE QUESTIONS

Write down your answers here:

1. Who did this?

   _____

2. What was their role?

   _____

3. Where did they work?

   _____

4. What did they do to you?

   _____

   _____

5. When did this happen?

   _____

   _____

6. Who did you tell?

   _____

7. Was it reported to a person of authority?

   _____

8. What did the institution do?

   _____

   _____

   _____

9. How has this impacted your life?

   _____

   _____

   _____

10. Were they criminally prosecuted?

    _____

    _____

If you'd like more information about sexual abuse, Assembly Bills, Fight for Survivors, or Greenberg Gross, you can scan this QR code and be taken to our website at FightForSurvivors.com.

FIGHTING TO FIX THE SYSTEM

Patricia had started going to the gym because she had eating disorders pretty much her whole life, and a doctor thought working with an expert trainer could help her beat her problem. Her gym introduced her to a trainer, Jeff, who claimed he was a registered nurse (turns out he wasn't) and knew about eating disorders.

Desperate to overcome her eating disorder once and for all, Patricia did whatever Jeff said to. He had her exercise in front of a mirror. She would cry and tell him she didn't want to.

"If you want to beat this, you have to," he told her.

That was his answer for everything. She didn't question it. She thought he was her friend.

After a few months, on April 4th, 2002, Jeff came to Patricia's house one day and told her he had a pill that would help her lose eight pounds within a week. He insisted she take it.

She reluctantly took it and drank the liquid Jeff handed her. It tasted like chocolate.

The next thing she knew, she felt woozy. Jeff helped her upstairs.

She woke to find him on top of her. He wrapped her face in saran wrap and began beating her with a bat and trying to murder her. He also threatened to kill her 12-year-old son, who was not home at the time.

All the while, Patricia made a promise to God: *Please don't take my life. If I live, with each and every next breath hereafter, I will live for the community above self.*

A Miraculous Escape

Patricia has a spotty memory of what happened next and is uncertain as to whether she jumped or was pushed off the 12-foot balcony of her upstairs loft. However, when she dropped and landed in her kitchen, she ran out of her front door and to the neighbor's door, banging and praying someone would answer. Finally, three doors later, a neighbor opened the door to find Patricia beaten, half-naked, and in shock.

The neighbor called the police immediately. Patrica was taken to a hospital, then transported to another hospital to have a rape kit done.

She wanted Jeff in jail so that he couldn't re-victimize her, hurt her son, or go on to hurt somebody else. Unfortunately, because the rape kit results were inconclusive and she had no memory of what had happened, the prosecutor said she couldn't prove a sexual assault case. Fortunately, there were still other crimes the DA could prove.

Jeff was charged with deliberate, premeditated attempted murder, burglary in the first degree, assault with a deadly weapon, and criminal threats.

An Unacceptable Outcome

Months later, Patricia received a call from a victim's advocate who said, "Patricia, you have half an hour. You need to get to court."

"What do you mean?" asked Patricia.

"Just get here now."

Patricia had been dealing with severe PTSD, anxiety, and depression. She hadn't worked since the assault and had lost all her savings because she could barely get out of bed. She had to force herself to get dressed and go to the court. She made it just in time to hear the judge say, "Okay, sentencing will be..." She turned to the advocate, confused.

"What's happening?"

"Don't worry. He admitted to everything. He wrote out an admission for the DA, and the DA accepted a two-year plea deal."

However, Patricia was worried. The sentence was paltry, and she knew it. He only received two years for what he had done to her! The system had failed her. Patricia knew she had to do something.

Fighting Back

She picketed the courthouse, and the judge withdrew the defendant's plea and set it for jury trial.

The judge made horrible rulings and removed some crimes for the jury's consideration. After the trial, the judge sentenced him to only 120 days in jail. Patricia reported the judge to the Judicial Commission. She spent thousands of dollars of her own money to order transcripts and study the law so she could get the judge off the bench for all the inappropriate comments and unjust rulings.

It worked. The judge was forced to retire. And Patricia didn't stop there. She decided she wasn't going to be a victim but a survivor. She sued Jeff and was awarded a $6 million judgment. The gym agreed to run background checks on their staff in exchange for Patricia not going after them civilly. She was happy with that, knowing it would help to prevent them from hiring predators in the future.

A Promise Kept

Patricia also kept her word from when she prayed on that terrible night. She would live for her community. She started an organization to help victims of crime, called Crime Survivors. She didn't want anyone to go through what she had been through, but she also didn't want anyone to think it was their fault if they were victimized. She wanted to help victims know that they're not alone — like how she had felt alone — and to help bring awareness, prevention, advocacy, and healing to communities.

Patricia had owned a successful catering business before her life fell apart after this violent assault, and thankfully, she knew how to run the new nonprofit like a business. She had the support of the local police and started with a big run-walk in the city of Irvine, California. She's been hosting this event annually ever since. Her organization puts on multiple fundraising events and community outreach programs to help survivors.

She built a resource center that now serves all of Southern California, helping survivors with whatever they need. They provide direct services, offer support for counseling and therapy, and have a peer-to-peer support group. They also hold classes on topics such as art-for-healing and safety/self-defense. They have holiday programming and much more. Whether victims need relocation, diapers, food, clothing, help to plan a funeral, media support — whatever they need — Patricia's organization can help.

READY TO SHARE YOUR STORY? HOW TO PREPARE FOR YOUR CALL

They collaborate with other local organizations too, such as victim advocates or local shelters for other services, including help locating housing.

Today, Patricia has helped thousands of victims. She credits helping others as being part of her own healing. While her work can be very challenging, she always tells survivors to find their passion and purpose. It doesn't have to be helping other survivors.

By living fully, you are taking back your life. And you are helping other victims to see what's possible. It gives them hope.

"I want victims to know that whatever darkness you have, there is a light to get through it," she said.

Patricia didn't receive justice in a criminal trial, even though the perpetrator was prosecuted. However, she did find it in a civil one. Civil litigation might just provide you with the justice, validation, recourse, and purpose you've been looking for when the criminal system falls short or even if you didn't pursue that path in the first place. And the financial damages can also help you rebuild your life while making a difference in your community.

By living fully, you are taking back your life.

If you're interested in donating to the Crime Survivors Resource Center and you want to learn more, visit CrimeSurvivors.org.

CHAPTER 7

IS IT WORTH IT?

ROBERT: A NIGHTMARE FINALLY ENDS

Forty-year-old Robert was enjoying a Sunday morning, reading the paper in his recliner, when his hands started to shake. He began sweating, and his heart sank into his stomach. He thought he was going to be sick.

He had just read that his fourth-grade teacher, Mr. Baker, had been arrested for abusing several boys.

"This nightmare is starting all over again," Robert thought as he crumbled the paper in his trembling hands.

Robert was now a happily married man with a loving son. However, he'd been keeping a horrible secret since he was nine years old, even from his wife: His teacher, Mr. Baker, used to keep him in a "think tank" after school. It was a corner designated for reading and "thinking" that was sold as a reward for getting homework done early in class. Mr. Baker would use the "think tank" to sexually abuse him in this hidden corner of the class after all the other students had left.

Robert dreaded getting called to the "think tank" and even stopped doing his homework, hoping it would keep him from having to go into that isolated part of the classroom. Unfortunately, that didn't work. The abuse continued, only stopping at the end of the school year when Robert began summer vacation. Unfortunately, though the abuse stopped, the pain, shame, and guilt did not.

After Robert grew up and went to college, his problems with drugs and alcohol started. He tried to numb the pain, escape the emotions, and drown out the swirling thoughts he continuously had about the abuse. For most of his 20s, Robert spun out of control.

He knew he had to address his issues. During his early 30s, he started searching for Mr. Baker. He thought maybe if he found him and saw what had become of him, perhaps it would bring him some peace. Maybe he had been caught.

A Horrible Discovery

That's when Robert discovered the unthinkable: Mr. Baker was working as a youth pastor in a large church. The idea that this horrible predator was a youth pastor was more than Robert could bear. Hands shaking, he called the church, having the courage to tell someone for the first time that their pastor had sexually abused him when he was a child.

"We just don't think he would do that," replied the voice at the other end of the phone. "But you can come and be interviewed."

Robert was stunned. He had never told anyone before because he thought he wouldn't be believed, and now his fears were coming true. Still, he knew the truth.

He mustered up the courage to go to the church and be interviewed. The church decided to remove Mr. Baker. Robert felt relieved. He had done what he couldn't do all those years ago and stopped the monster.

Anxiety Returns

With a new lease on life, Robert got clean and sober with the help of AA. He met a wonderful woman, and they had a baby. He thought his troubles were behind him until he read the paper that Sunday morning and realized he hadn't stopped the monster. The monster had simply moved on.

It turns out that after he was kicked out of the church, Mr. Baker just moved on and got a job at another school. The school never asked questions about why the church had kicked him out or even where he had been for the past two years. It was when he was at that job that he was arrested.

Robert was spiraling into depression and anxiety. He called the detective listed in the newspaper, courageously telling his story again, hopeful he could finally get some justice for all the abuse he had endured.

"I'm sorry," replied the detective. "Your case was so long ago that it falls outside the statute of limitations. However, we could still use your help."

The DA was assembling people to testify as corroborating witnesses because Mr. Baker had gone on and abused several more children. They asked Robert to testify in the criminal trial.

Can I get up there and face this guy after all these years? Robert wondered.

He knew he had to, so he agreed. He still felt guilty for not saying anything sooner, but he had to try to make it right.

Making Things Right

During the case, when Robert was finally called as a witness, he didn't even look at Mr. Baker. This was about the other boys. He was here for them. Robert was sweaty, and his heart was palpitating. As it turned out, though, the overall questioning wasn't as awful as he feared. There was only one question that made him break down in tears.

"If this really happened, why didn't you come forward as a child?" asked the defense attorney.

Robert paused, his eyes welling up. "Fear. The fear of getting in trouble. The fear of being branded as a tattletale that got a teacher fired. That the kids would say I was gay. The fears I had as a child now seem silly, but they felt very real when I was young."

Robert was asked to step down. Two hours after the case was submitted to the jury, Mr. Baker was declared guilty. He received a sentence of 20 years in prison.

They believed me! Robert thought.

A wave of relief came over him. The monster would be behind bars. The nightmare was finally over... or so he thought.

A Difficult Choice

Robert still struggled — and this struggle, too, was in silence. He had managed to keep everything from his wife. She didn't know anything about the trial or Mr. Baker.

The guilt about not coming forward sooner persisted. He didn't feel like he got his own justice, and he still hated that the school was never held accountable. He rarely slept, experienced terrible migraines, and started drinking heavily again.

His wife didn't recognize the man she was married to anymore. She couldn't understand why he was drinking so much. She told him he had to choose either alcohol or his family.

Robert got clean and sober once again and got his life back on track. He still didn't tell his wife about what had happened to him, but she saw his progress despite his inner turmoil. They became a family again.

Still, what had happened to him continued to torment him. Many years after Mr. Baker was convicted, Robert, now in his late 40s, called us to see if anything more could be done. He had read about the statute of limitations changing and wanted to know if he had a civil case. He did.

"Is this something you think you'd like to pursue?" I asked.

"I don't know," he said. "I'm so ashamed I didn't say anything sooner. I think about all those boys I could have saved if I had just spoken up sooner."

Robert was scared. His life was finally back on track, and he was afraid of opening old wounds that might cause him to spiral again.

"Let me tell you how I see it," I said. "When we go after one perpetrator, sure, we get the bad guy. We've saved a few kids, and that's wonderful. However, when we go after the schools that let the bad guy in, we ensure they don't allow it to happen again. We save hundreds, if not thousands, of kids in future generations."

"Wow, I never thought about it that way," said Robert. He paused. "But I can't afford an attorney."

That's when I explained to him that these cases are done on a contingency basis, with no upfront or out-of-pocket costs for him.

"You could finally get justice," I said. "YOU deserve justice."

I told him to think about it and also referred him to a therapist. He thanked me and said he'd be in touch.

When he hung up, Robert couldn't shake all his old fears. *Will they believe me? What if I spiral out of control again? What will I tell my wife?*

That last one stuck with him. He knew if he was going to do this, he had to find the courage to finally tell his wife about the demons that had haunted him. So, after all these years, he told her.

She was nothing but kind and understanding and just so sad that he had suffered alone for so many years. She wanted to support him in whatever he needed.

The Final Resolution

A few days later, Robert called me back. "I want in." We filed a civil lawsuit on his behalf.

When the deposition day came, he was scared, thoughts swirling in his head. However, as it turned out, it was that deposition that finally freed him from his emotional prison. He finally was able to tell his whole story. Even the attorney on the other side was in tears as Robert recounted his entire story, including what happened and how it affected his life and his family.

The school district settled for multi-millions. Robert had the money he needed to support him on his road to recovery and can now spend as much time with his family as he wants. He had finally put his demons to rest.

ARE THE EMOTIONAL COSTS WORTH THE PURSUIT?

Victims often try to weigh the emotional cost of revisiting old wounds versus just keeping silent.

Even if you have told other people what happened to you, going to court and telling it again is an entirely different situation.

If you've told others and experienced the resulting sense of relief and healing, you might worry that a lawsuit will only reopen the old wounds and bring you pain again. You're not sure it's worth it.

However, the cost of not doing it can definitely be higher.

As one research study puts it, "Trauma is an emotional response to a terrible event."[8] It's completely understandable why we don't want to keep having those responses. Sometimes, we feel overwhelmed, and we break down if we talk about a painful experience for too long. Some people believe if they're not having a full breakdown, the trauma hasn't really affected them.

I know I felt that way when I was younger. I thought I was doing just fine, letting it go and moving forward, thinking I'd let time heal those wounds.

Unfortunately, as we explored in Chapter 4, time doesn't heal trauma wounds. Over and over again, Robert thought he was fine and that he had finally put it all behind him. But, over and over, the emotional trauma came back up, manifesting as self-destructive behaviors. It wasn't until he felt like he had finally been able to do something to prevent this from ever happening again that he found mental and physical freedom.

Standing up and speaking up against evil is probably the greatest thing that you can do, not only for your own healing but for others. Once you share your story, you are going to empower other survivors of the same perpetrator (or from the same school district) to come forward. I'll say it again: Where there's one victim of sexual assault, there are always more. Most child molesters have upwards of ten to 100 different victims. You are not alone, not just because you're not the only person who's ever been molested, but the perpetrator who sexually assaulted you always has more victims. If you become older or move away, they just move on to other students.

Schools and institutions have a legal duty and obligation to keep children safe from the people entrusted with their care. We can stop responsible authorities from turning a blind eye and not noticing. It's worth speaking up because there's nothing more worthwhile than helping a child.

> *We can stop responsible authorities from turning a blind eye and not noticing.*

WHY NOW? AND HOW?

Often, survivors of childhood sexual abuse don't address it until later in life, even just a few years later, when they're able to understand it better.

The average age at which someone discloses childhood sexual abuse and assault for the first time is 52.[9] One of the reasons so many people come to us later in life is because they learned of the change in the statute of limitations for a civil case, they've thought about this for so long, or are finally trying to address the root causes of their self-destructive behaviors, physical ailments, or problems in their relationships.

Perhaps this is where you are in your situation, too.

If you are now an adult with your own children, they might be in the age range that you were in when you were abused. You may experience intrusive thoughts, wondering if your child's teacher is a molester. Reliving the abuse becomes paralyzing. Even if you believe your children's teachers to be safe, it still makes you start to think about how your own school failed to protect you. You want to finally do something to protect other students, including your children.

If you're a young adult, your situation may be different. Like many young people who come forward, you could be in the middle of some other type of emotional crisis. Unfortunately, defense attorneys will try to use that against you, saying you're lying to get out of the trouble you're currently facing. We use expert witnesses in these cases to explain that younger people commonly disclose their abuse when they're in the midst of an emotional crisis and that they also commonly engage in self-destructive behaviors because of the abuse.

If you're currently going through puberty, the topic may have come up with a partner who is asking if you've done something before, and the question reminds you of your abuse. As a teenager, you are starting to find the tools to process what happened to you and find yourself confiding it either to a romantic partner or a close friend. This is called "delayed disclosure," and it's also something we address with an expert witness.

No matter what your age, maybe you've decided to come forward because you've realized the abuse is going to happen to someone else if you don't. You've been suffering in silence, but now you've seen your abuser talking to your cousin or another kid, and the desire to protect someone else has taken over. This is one of the most common reasons for disclosure, and it's the same motivation for filing a civil case — to help prevent this from happening to anyone else.

GIVING POWER BACK TO THE POWERLESS

Victims feel powerless. There is a literal imbalance of power in childhood sexual assault with an adult perpetrator. Before fully disclosing their abuse, the victim might first test the waters by telling a trusted adult a small thing, such as saying a coach creeps them out. If the adult dismisses them or tones down the child's concern, the child feels more powerless and resolves to not tell the bigger truth, the whole truth.

As the victim ages, they become almost locked into that powerlessness. It's very hard for them to trust other people because they couldn't trust their parents or the school district to protect them. They certainly couldn't trust the teacher entrusted to protect them if that teacher was the perpetrator, and the victim couldn't trust the other teachers if those teachers suspected something was "off" but did nothing.

For those of us helping to fight for survivors, the best way to help someone who has confided in you about being abused is to listen, let them know you believe them, assure them that it is not their fault, and accompany them to any medical or legal appointments. Praise them for being courageous enough to trust you with their story, and try to empower them going forward.

THE MONETARY COST

A lot of people don't want to bring a civil suit because they think they can't afford an attorney. However, when you go after an institution for money, you don't have to pay the civil lawyers up front. Most law firms will take cases on what's called a contingency basis. Any costs that are incurred along the way, like hiring expert witnesses or taking depositions, are paid for by the law firm and get reimbursed out of any settlement or successful jury verdict. If the case is unsuccessful, the law firm does not recoup the costs it incurred to litigate, and you would not owe your law firm any money for the time it spent on your case. However, depending on the rules in the state you file in, the court may require you to pay costs and/or fees to the opposing party. It is, therefore, imperative that you consult with an attorney with regard to the specific laws within your state.

Before the trial begins, the law firm will sign a contract with the survivor for a fee-split agreement. Normally, the law firm gets 40 percent of the settlement after the trial, minus any costs. If the survivor is still a child, the law may require the percentage to be lower.

YOUR EXPERIENCE DOES NOT DEFINE YOU

One of the reasons adults don't want to come forward is because they don't want to be "branded" and have this horrible event define them. They don't want people to pity them, treat them differently, or think they're damaged.

You are not broken. In fact, by speaking up, you become stronger than ever. Many well-known people have shared their stories of childhood sexual abuse and transformed their experiences into protection and healing for others.

If someone thinks that you're broken because you are a survivor who took control of your life, do you really care about what that person thinks?

I don't see myself as broken. I see myself as a warrior in the fight to prevent child sexual abuse. The broken ones are the ones who didn't do anything to prevent it or covered it up when they were made aware of it.

As I said in Chapter 4, you can be referred to as John Doe or Jane Doe during a case if you want to protect your identity. You get to decide. You get to control the narrative. You have the power.

What happened to you does not define you. You decide what it means. If every survivor was able to stand up and shine a light into the darkness, we could change the world.

If every survivor was able to stand up and shine a light into the darkness, we could change the world.

CHAPTER 8

TURNING PAIN INTO PURPOSE

It won't make a difference.
It'll take too much time.
I don't have the energy to go through this.
Money won't change what happened.
What's the point?

I have heard it all. A thousand thoughts and questions can have clients wondering: Why go through a trial?

As I have said so many times, by going through a civil trial, you can help prevent this from happening in the future. After a civil trial, schools are compelled to make changes to prevent similar incidents from happening. They can no longer sweep things under the rug, or worse, cover them up. Sure, you can get some money to help you, but the return on your investment is on a much grander global level of actually fighting for other people. Nothing will fill your soul more than knowing you helped to prevent abuse from happening to multiple children.

Survivors often forget about the power of corroboration. Coming forward helps give other people who might have been victims (and there is never just one) the courage to say, "He did this to me, too." When people know they are not the only ones and that other people care enough to step forward, they feel safe coming forward, too.

And when you win the case? You will feel a great deal of strength and freedom, which will leave you astonished. You will become a leader, inspiring other people by showing them what it looks like to really stand up for something bigger than you. Yes, this was a major bump in the road. However, once you're past it, you will become a better version of yourself to live your best life. You will stop spinning your wheels inward and start looking out to connect with others. You will help other survivors feel less alone, and you will feel less alone.

THE SPECTRUM OF IMPACT

I have said before that I know that no amount of money can ever change what happened to you or the survivor you are supporting. But, as I've also said before, what it can do is help you deal with the damage this event might have inflicted on your life. Making institutions pay for the damage they've allowed on their watch is what creates the change.

When their monetary reserves are depleted, their insurance rates go up, or their reputation is damaged in a way that could impact their future; they will not want to experience that situation again. The legal action puts the school on notice that people are watching, so they better safeguard our children going forward.

As I have said, most civil cases settle out of court, so it might not take as much time or effort as you imagine. I have seen instances where just filing a demand letter on a school district compelled them to make a settlement offer. It doesn't happen often, but it is possible. We had a case involving a performing arts school in which a teacher played favorites and would make some really inappropriate comments, including a suggestive, highly derogatory and embarrassing one made about a young female in his class as she left to go to the bathroom. In that situation, once we sent the demand letter, the school had no choice but to let him go and resolve the case.

Change is already happening. I have seen more and more people come forward, and it's the people who have come before you and dared to speak up that brought forth new legislation. Right now, more laws are in place than ever before to protect survivors, and more are yet to come. All the new state assembly bills are the result of legislators beginning to understand the long-lasting effects of the trauma and seeing a need for change. With more and more people sharing their stories and experiences, our legislatures recognize the huge collateral damage these types of crimes bring, both to victims and to society as a whole. Many states have expanded the litigation windows because they now

More laws are in place than ever before to protect survivors, and more are yet to come.

understand that the victims are simply in survival mode for a while and not in any position to even think about civilly litigating something right away.

Public awareness has also expanded. People who once might not have wanted to believe these things could happen in their schools now realize they occur more often than one could imagine. That awareness of the pervasiveness of this issue makes parents and educators more conscious and vigilant. It's giving them the strength to confront school districts and other institutions to compel them to do better and put programs in place to help children.

ERIN'S LAW

In 2013, Illinois became the first state to pass Erin's Law. It requires all public schools to implement a sexual abuse awareness and prevention curriculum for grades Pre-K to 12. Thirty-eight states have now passed Erin's Law. Erin Merryn, the law's namesake, is now trying to get it passed in all 50 states.

Erin is a childhood sexual assault survivor, author, speaker, and activist. She created Erin's Law to help other victims.

While she was between the ages of six and eight and a half, Erin's best friend's uncle, who was also her neighbor, abused her. It first started at a sleepover. Threatened the whole time, she kept it a secret but started acting out and was labeled an emotionally disturbed child.

She had to repeat first grade. She received all sorts of services from the school and was on an individual education plan (IEP). They had her engage in programs to help her with her anger.

The abuse only ended when her family moved. All the acting out and other problems also disappeared when they moved. They removed her from any special programs, and things seemed to return to normal. She made new friends, but she never wanted to sleep over at their houses, which her parents found odd. They just figured she was a homebody because she only wanted to do sleepovers at their own home.

A Shattered Family

What Erin didn't know was that there was also a predator in her own family. At the age of 11, she woke up to her teenage cousin Brian abusing her while she was spending the night at her grandparents' house. Again, she didn't tell anyone. She started keeping a diary and would write in it almost every day. When she was 12, she was playing hide and seek at her aunt and uncle's house when that same cousin said he would help her hide. Instead, he took her to the basement to abuse her. He also threatened her to keep it a secret, saying no one would believe her. Again, Erin didn't tell anyone. She just kept writing in her diary. The abuse continued happening whenever her family was together for holidays.

This time, Erin's grades dropped, and she became depressed. She also had other health problems that required her to have an operation, so the family just thought that was what was making her depressed.

One evening, Erin's sister came to her and said, "Brian's gross." It was then that she realized he was abusing her sister, too.

Erin and her sister told their parents what was happening the very next day. Their parents told Brian's parents what was happening, but when confronted, Brian denied it. Erin's extended family took his side. Her parents just wanted to get him some help, but everyone refused to even talk about it because they couldn't believe it was possible. Her cousin had been right. It destroyed their family. Erin's immediate family didn't see the rest of them anymore.

Erin's parents reported what had happened to the police. She and her sister were taken to a Children's Advocacy Center (CAC) and interviewed by a forensic interviewer. They brought Brian in, and while being interviewed, he confessed. Brian was put under arrest. After all this, the rest of the family stuck by Brian, still not believing Erin and her sister.

The authorities told Erin's parents they had a choice. Either they could have a trial, and she and her sister would have to take the stand against him, or they could do what they originally wanted, which was to get him treatment. The detective made it sound like if they went forward with prosecution, Erin and her sister would definitely end up having to get on the stand to testify. Their parents didn't want that. Brian was instead screened through juvenile court. He did not face any jail time but had to go through some sex offender treatment, a thousand hours of community service, and be on probation.

Continued Suffering

Erin's parents were content. They wanted their kids to move on with their lives. Erin and her sister ended up getting excellent help and care through a support group at the Children's Advocacy Center. CACs are nonprofits, so all the services were free.

Still, Erin suffered. She was depressed and had anxiety and PTSD. She ended up going down a self-destructive path in high school that included self-harm and a suicide attempt at 16. It wasn't until her junior year of high school that a therapist said, "You have so much anger toward your cousin. If you had the opportunity to speak to him, what would you say to him? Why don't you try writing a letter?"

Erin went home and wrote a five-page letter. The assignment wasn't to send it to him, but she looked up his email and did it anyway. She wanted answers: "Why did you do this to my sister? Were you abused? What were you thinking?"

In the end, Erin's cousin couldn't really explain why he did what he did, claiming it was just "sexual curiosity," but he was remorseful and wanted forgiveness. When she got that final letter from him, seven months after they started corresponding, something in her opened up. She realized she could continue to allow his actions to rob her of her joy and happiness, or she could do something positive.

Taking Charge

Now a senior in high school, Erin decided to write a book. She pulled up her old diary and started typing. She kept a lot of it word for word, wanting to keep things in the voice of a child, a teenager. Erin completed her book *Stolen Innocence* right before she graduated and self-published it. Six months later, when she was away at college, a publishing company bought the rights from her to publish it.

It was also in college that Erin finally disclosed to her parents what had happened with her neighbor, starting when she was six. Her parents were so distraught over what her cousin did that she felt like she could never tell them about what the neighbor had done.

However, by now, she also had an eating disorder, and they were getting on her case about not eating, so Erin broke down. Her parents called the police, who went and found that old neighbor. He was still living in the same place with his sister, who kicked him out that night, even though he flat-out denied the accusations. He wouldn't cooperate with law enforcement, and because there was no physical evidence, the case never went anywhere.

Erin did confront him, though. She wrote him a letter, and his sister, who was always in Erin's corner, hand-delivered the letter. Erin never got a response. However, she is still in touch with her abuser's sister, who says he is in poor health and on weekly kidney dialysis. His sister believes he is paying now for what he did.

And Erin wasn't done. As a child, she had to go through tornado drills, bus drills, fire drills, DARE (Drug Abuse Resistance Education), and had learned all about stranger danger. Yet she learned later in life that 90 percent of the time, kids are being abused by someone they know and trust.[10] No one had taught her how to speak up and tell. Why hadn't someone been educating her on this?

So, in 2007, she wrote to her state senator. He actually agreed that kids needed personal body safety education but thought a bill like that would never get passed. She wrote back: "That's why it needs to change in our society.

We don't talk about this. We look the other way. And if you won't help me, I will find somebody that will."

Teaching Self-Protection

It took her almost three years, but in 2011, Erin was able to enlist the help of the new state senator, Tim Bivins. Erin's Law was introduced in 2011 in Illinois, and it passed in 2013. Once a year, from kindergarten through twelfth grade, kids are taught about safe and unsafe touch, safe and unsafe secrets, and who are the safe adults to go to when reporting. They are taught that if they are being abused and they speak up, they'll be believed.

Erin continued the good fight, and after almost 14 years as of writing this, Erin's Law has been passed in 38 states. It has even been passed in Kerala, India and is about to be passed in Ontario, Canada. It is credited with hundreds, if not thousands, of kids coming forward.

Erin receives letters all the time from people all over the country. A mother in Georgia wrote to her and said, "I can't thank you enough. I've never talked to my kids about this. My daughter learned about your law in school, and she came home the day after her birthday and told me that when her grandfather, my husband's father, took her out for her birthday, he had abused her multiple times in the car.

"He is being prosecuted in two different counties because he took her to another county and abused her in the parking lot in his car," the letter went on. "I read your book and learned how your abuse destroyed your family. It has destroyed our family too, as my husband's father was his hero.

We have been isolated from the rest of our family, too. But your story is giving us strength to fight and heal together."

It's those kinds of letters that keep Erin fighting, too. New York killed her bill for eight years due to a state representative who was the chair of the education committee and against school mandates. Instead of giving up, Erin just kept coming back to the floor; at times she had her infant daughter in tow when she needed to meet with lawmakers. Eventually, that chair stepped down, and the new chair stepped in to be a champion to get Erin's Law to the finish line.

In June 2019, Erin's Law was passed in New York and signed into law by the governor in August. It went into effect in the fall of 2020 for the school year. That spring, nine boys in a school upstate came forward saying they were being sexually abused by their principal. The principal had a "lunch buddies program" where the "buddy" would have lunch alone with him. During the trial, 27 boys, some of whom were 19 years old now, testified that they had been molested by him throughout their elementary school years. When he was convicted and received 63 years in prison, the superintendent went on the news and said this would have never happened without Erin's Law.

Erin's Law Foundation

Erin recently created a 501(c)3 non-profit organization called Erin's Law Foundation. It allows her to translate the curriculum into multiple languages and offer it for free. She will be able to provide the curriculum right on her website to help any parent or educator. Her next project is to provide college scholarships to high school students who are survivors. And she is also working on offering different retreats for adult survivors.

Erin travels the country, speaking at conferences and different schools, sharing something she was always told to keep quiet about. She took something that for years ate away at her and made it her life mission. It could have sent her on a completely different path, and she did struggle for a period of time, but she turned it around and did something about it to help others. She is a warrior, a fighter, and a hero.

You don't have to create new laws, new curriculum, or go on a speaking tour to make a difference. However, you can speak up about what happened to you, if nothing more than for your own personal healing and growth. Sometimes, the worst things that happen to us can lead us to our greatest purpose.

Sometimes, the worst things that happen to us can lead us to our greatest purpose.

If you're interested in donating to the Erin's Law Foundation and learning more, please visit ErinsLaw.org.

CHAPTER 9

WHAT DO YOU NEED MOST RIGHT NOW?

I've gone through so much in my life. The story I've told you about myself in this book is just the tip of the iceberg. However, none of the bad things that happened to me define me. I have found that what actually defines me is my resilience despite my struggles and setbacks.

Freeing and healing myself started with my speaking about all the things I've had to overcome. And empowering other sexual assault survivors — letting them know that they're not alone and that they are doing something incredibly powerful to change the world by standing up against evil — has given me so much more purpose and satisfaction in my life than I could ever have imagined. I went from feeling empty to overflowing with gratitude. I went from being angry about what happened to me to seeing it as a tool to be used for good.

I don't want anyone to have to suffer what I suffered through or what any of the survivors in this book suffered through. I don't want this to happen to any more children. In my career, I have seen too much pain and wreckage. I've seen lives that have spun out of control — victims who can't hold a job or have fulfilling marriages, those with alcohol and drug addictions, those who go on to have a lifetime fear of intimacy, and sometimes much more. Yet, I have also seen the light that comes from people who have used their voices to stand up against evil. That sense of purpose can transform you.

I no longer resent the abuse I suffered as a child. I no longer feel guilty about not coming forward sooner. It no longer has power over me but has become my greatest strength in helping others to find their way to heal and obtain justice.

What about you? How would you like to feel empowered, to gain peace with yourself? To let go of the guilt, the shame, the feeling of powerlessness?

Child sexual abuse is a horrible experience, and you've suffered from it, in whatever way, through the rest of your life. You may have resigned yourself to never having peace with your experience. You may have felt powerless and unable to change your situation.

And yet, what if you could?

WHAT KIND OF WORLD DO YOU WANT?

This is a global crisis, and if we want to do anything to effect real change, we all need to be in the fight. We need more people willing to use their voices.

What kind of story would you like to create for yourself? Do you want a story in which you were the victim, powerless and afraid, or would you prefer the story of you as a hero, helping to save other children from suffering at the hands of predators?

Do you want schools and other institutions to remain blind to what's going on under their noses, or do you want them to be vigilant in protecting the children in their care?

Do you want abusers to get away with their actions because too many people are afraid to speak out, or do you want to take charge and tell your story, perhaps giving others the courage to do the same?

Together, we are powerful. Together, we can rise up against this epidemic and defeat the darkness.

YOUR PEACE IS IMPORTANT

In this book, you've read the stories of people who were finally able to go from being survivors still battling the effects of their trauma to becoming heroes and warriors making the choice to obtain justice and find real healing.

It wasn't until they took action against those who let them be abused that they could finally get relief.

Think about the way in which your experience with child sexual abuse has affected your life. Do you have mental health issues that could be related to what happened? Are you able to have healthy relationships? Do you suffer from physical ailments that could be signs of repressed trauma?

If taking a stand against your abuser could help you relieve some of these things, is it worth taking the chance?

YOU'RE ARMED FOR ACTION

You're aware now of how the court system works and what your options are. You even have a list of the questions to start thinking about, so you're ready to answer them.

Hopefully, you know enough about the U.S. court system to now be aware that money won't be an obstacle since a civil case is paid on contingency. You know what kind of litigation team to look for — civil litigators specializing in child sexual assault.

You've got a good idea of how the process of filing a lawsuit would work and how our SHINE process takes clients through that. If you're not in California, you can look for a team that will help you through your state's process in their own way, and you'll have the SHINE process to compare it to so you can make sure they'll give you everything you need.

You also now know that you most likely won't even have to go to trial if you do decide to move forward. In the unlikely event that you do have a trial, you'll have a team of people to support you through the whole process.

No one needs to give you permission to make the decision. You have everything you need to move forward. You have control. You can decide for yourself.

Instead of asking whether it will be worth it, let's ask a different question. What happens if you don't do anything at all?

WHAT IF YOU DECIDE NOT TO DO ANYTHING?

No one can force you to do anything about any of this. If you decide to just forget about it and move on, what happens?

Your life stays the same. You continue dealing with your own issues as you have. If your life is already great, and you don't want to rock that boat, I get it.

If the perpetrator is still alive and not in prison, he or she will probably still be doing the same things to others. If the organization you were in is still around, the people within it may still be missing what they missed with you. They may still be failing to protect those in their charge.

And yet, if you can imagine a better future for yourself and others, what would it look like? Sometimes, it's not so easy to see that future from where you're sitting because you get used to just accepting where you are.

Think about Debbie. She struggled with her emotions so much after her abuse that she never really settled down or felt happy. Before her settlement, could she have imagined doing anything like buying a house or going to school? What about Robert, who had suffered for so many long years and hadn't even told his wife? Could he have imagined a future free from substance abuse and mental illness? Mandy finally got to go to college and went on to help at-risk youth. Would she ever have imagined this opportunity when she was younger and believed she had no options for justice?

When you are engulfed by the darkness of despair and confusion, hope seems far away. It is difficult to imagine anything beyond your day-to-day existence as you know it.

Let someone help you see differently.

With faith and courage (and maybe a miracle or two), you can achieve things that will surprise you. Faith and courage are vital in defeating darkness.

YOUR EXPERIENCE IS ALSO YOUR STRENGTH

You can use the very thing that caused you pain for good in your life. You can turn the thing you're most ashamed and resentful of into your greatest purpose.

Who better to help someone going through a divorce than someone who's gone through a divorce? Who better to help someone with an addiction than someone who's struggled with addiction? Who better to help someone going through cancer than someone who's gone through cancer?

Your strength is in your voice. By speaking up, you let other victims (especially of the same perpetrator) know they are not alone and can help protect others in the future. They will hear you because you already hear them.

Free yourself from those swirling thoughts. Help pull others out of their pain. Hold the people who should have protected you accountable for what happened and require them to do better in the future. Educate those in charge to keep a watchful eye on those around them. Use your voice.

HOW TO GET STARTED

If you feel ready to speak up, first of all, know that I am so proud of you.

If you're wondering where to begin, answer the questions in Chapter 6 and find someone to talk to. Even if you tell someone and they don't know exactly what to say, they can listen. When I finally told my mom about my abuse all those years later, her outrage gave me comfort. She believed me.

You don't have to live with these secrets any longer. Even if you aren't ready to call the police or an attorney, call a therapist or a friend. Your friends can be surprisingly compassionate. If you don't have a close friend or family member to tell (or you're not ready), call a therapist. Choose a therapist who knows how to deal with sexual trauma, and they can give you some great tools. Heck, you can call me if you need to, but just tell someone.

This first step alone will do so much to help free your soul. Every time you release bits and pieces of the secret that you've been holding onto and shoving down deep inside, it gets easier. The sooner you can talk, the sooner you can begin to heal.

By just starting and taking this first step, you are beginning to defeat the darkness, both for yourself and to prevent this from happening to someone else.

Don't let your abuse be in vain. There is nothing you can do to undo it, but you have the power to turn it into something used for good. You can be the light in the darkness that another person needs, and by standing up to fight for yourself and for others, you can emerge victorious.

APPENDIX

INFORMATION FOR PARENTS AND TEACHERS

If you are a parent or teacher, you're already helping just by taking the time to read this book and learning more about the topic of child sexual abuse. We have a long way to go, but the more people like you who are aware and on guard, the better off our children and our society will be. In this section are some resources to help you protect children wherever you are.

BE AWARE OF FALSE FRIENDS

If you are a parent or a teacher, be like Rebecca. Keep a watchful eye on those adults around you.

Perpetrators aren't often total strangers jumping out of the bushes. Only 7 percent of child sexual abuse is perpetrated by strangers.[11] Almost all child sexual abuse is perpetrated by someone you and your child know, love, and trust.

Always take notice of an adult who has befriended you (and your spouse) but seems more interested in building a relationship with your child. They might not be deviant, but they are still worth questioning. The ultimate goal of grooming is forming an emotional connection with the child and reducing the child's inhibitions to prepare them for sexual activity. It's also to gain their trust and care to prevent them from reporting.

AVOID GIVING CONFUSING MESSAGES

As adults, we can unknowingly send the wrong messages to our children.

For instance, don't only teach your kids about "Stranger Danger." By telling a child not to trust strangers, parents are implicitly saying that it's OK to trust people they may know more casually, such as a teacher or a coach. We know strangers aren't the only potentially dangerous people.

Another example is when we encourage children to kiss a family member goodbye. Encouraging them to do it despite their protests questions their boundaries. It gives them the message that we think that family member is safe (even if they're not).

Children will often test the waters and try to tell someone that they are uncomfortable with an abuser's behavior. When a child talks about not liking it when a coach touches them at practice, but their parents wave it away as "just what guys in sports do," the parents send the message that we don't believe what's bothering our child is valid. We need to take children's concerns and boundaries seriously — before things can evolve.

WATCH FOR GROOMING BEHAVIORS

Watch out for an adult who does any of the following grooming activities:

- Gives gifts, such as snacks, baseball cards, or money.
- Provides rides home or to and from practices, school, and events alone or gives special privileges.
- Points out to the parent when the child lies; this gives them plausible deniability when and if the child does report the abuse.
- Initiates opportunities to be alone with one or more children.
- Makes inappropriate jokes and/or talks about sex, even under the guise of education; this is normalizing sexual talk.
- Teases a child about breast and genital development.
- Caters to the interest of a child, so the child will initiate contact with the perpetrator.
- Contacts the child outside of school hours, unless in a group message.
- Tickles or "accidentally" touches genitalia; coaches who normalize massage.
- Shows a child sexually explicit images.
- Takes pictures of children in underwear, bathing suits, dance wear, etc.

- Teaches children to keep secrets from their parents.
- Allows them to do things parents wouldn't, like drink, smoke, or watch dirty movies. This allows the perpetrator to "get something on" the child, so the child is then afraid they will get busted if they tell parents about the abuse.
- Engages in tactile stimulation, which feels good, so "good touch, bad touch" conversations don't work and bring the child more shame, so they won't talk.

Suspicious Signs

Teachers or caregivers, in particular, need to be aware of important signs:

- Be alert to the "favorite" teacher, the fun teacher, or the one who likes to "hang out" with the students during lunch or after school.
- If you find students, or one student, hanging out with a teacher outside of class, take notes, ask questions, and keep a watchful eye.
- If you see a coach or teacher engaging in inappropriate behavior (touching, making sexual comments, or engaging in "too friendly" behavior), tell someone! Even if it ends up being innocent, it is better to be safe than sorry.
- If you see something problematic, say something. It doesn't have to be confrontational. If you see a teacher get in a sleeping bag with a student, you can tell them it doesn't look good, and they should stop for their own protection. You can act like

- you're doing them a favor to stop it, and later, you should report it.
- Take a course on how to identify perpetrators and grooming.

Predators need access to their prey, which is why parents, teachers, coaches, and anyone who works with children needs to be especially vigilant. They need to keep their eyes and ears open and recognize the warning signs.

ARM YOUR CHILD WITH KNOWLEDGE

When my son was 14, he had a baseball coach that gave me the heebie-jeebies. Something just didn't sit right with me. I noticed he played favorites, and I was suspicious of how often he wanted to have more practice with my son. He still coached even though his school-aged son was no longer on the team. I purposefully watched him at every barbeque and ball game and made sure my son never went to anything he was sponsoring if I wasn't there to watch.

I may have been an overprotective mother, but I didn't care. My son was not going to fall prey to anyone on my watch. I flat-out told my son that I didn't trust that coach and that I wanted him to be on the lookout for his teammates. Even if my son had been eight instead of 14, I would have had a similar yet age-appropriate conversation with him.

It's important to arm your children with knowledge and share this knowledge in a way that doesn't scare them or put them in the position of bearing the burden of protecting themselves from predators. Be sure to teach your children how to avoid possible dangers and what to do if they find themselves in a potentially threatening situation. By doing this, you will empower them to know what to do in the event you are not there to protect them.

What to Tell Your Child

Talk about touch. Most parents forget that there is not only a power differential between the perpetrator and the child but that your child is often quite fond of the perpetrator. You need to teach your child that some adults have a problem with touching children. Explain to them that if an adult ever touches them in their private areas (and use specific terms like "breasts," "buttocks," etc.), it's important they tell you what's happening so you can help the adult with their problem regarding touching. This will take away any fear of getting someone they like or even love into trouble.

Don't teach them "good touch, bad touch" because this is vague, and sometimes the sexual activity comes with feeling good physically, and this can be confusing and lead to shame. Tell your child, "Even if it feels good, someone touching your private parts or having you touch theirs means they need help, so tell me so I can help."

Secrets don't apply. Teach your child to tell you if someone is threatening them or their family, even if the person says they'll get in trouble if they say anything. Let them know they will never get in trouble for telling a "secret" because secrets don't apply to your family.

Eliminate vulnerabilities. Send your children to summer day camps with their swimsuits on and sunscreen applied. This limits the amount of time your child needs to be naked and limits any excuses to touch your child. Tell them they should use a buddy system when going to the bathroom to change. Or, tell them ways to change without anyone being present, like changing in a bathroom stall instead of a locker room before practice.

Give them permission to not go along with what all the other kids do. Don't allow coaches and teachers to give your children rides to and from practices and or games. Keep this as a hard and fast rule that applies to everyone.

WHAT TO DO IF SOMEONE DISCLOSES TO YOU

Be supportive if someone discloses sexual abuse to you or even just tests the waters and tells you about something that makes them uncomfortable. Don't freak out or ask them, "Why didn't you tell me this was happening?" That will add to the guilt or imply that you think they are lying. Instead, just listen and stay calm. Say you believe them and thank them for trusting you with such a heavy secret they've been carrying.

If the perpetrator is someone you know and trust, don't confront them! Wait until you can get the victim in a safe environment and report the abuse to the authorities as soon as possible. If you confront the perpetrator immediately, you may hinder any criminal investigation going forward.

Seek professional help. Take your child to a therapist, telling the child you want them to have a safe place to speak about the abuse, that you are going to support them and get them the help they need, and that you will get through it together. Be sure to let the child know that you love them, that they did nothing wrong, and that you believe them! Their biggest fear was telling you. Your reaction with nothing but love and support can make all the difference in their healing journey.

In a nutshell:

- Acknowledge and support: "Thank you for trusting me with what's been happening. You did nothing wrong, and I'm proud of you for having the courage to say something. You are not in any trouble, and this is not your fault. I believe you, love you, support you, and will help and protect you."
- Call the authorities.
- Seek a therapist.
- Call Fight for Survivors (that's us): When the emotional dust settles from any potential criminal investigation, think about the relationship of the perpetrator and how they were able to gain access to you or a loved one. Was a school involved? An institution? Should they have known? Do you know of any other victims?

ENDNOTES

1. Prevent Child Abuse America, "Child Sexual Abuse Prevention," accessed June 11, 2024, https://preventchildabuse.org/what-we-do/child-sexual-abuse-prevention/.
2. Indiana Center for Prevention of Youth Abuse & Suicide, "Child Abuse Statistics," 2009-2022, https://www.indianaprevention.org/child-abuse-statistics.
3. Elizabeth L. Jeglic Ph.D., "Why Children Don't Tell Anyone About Sexual Abuse," Psychology Today, February 28, 2022, https://www.psychologytoday.com/us/blog/protecting-children-sexual-abuse/202202/why-children-don-t-tell-anyone-about-sexual-abuse.
4. Cornell Law School Legal Information Institute, "g," accessed June 11, 2024, https://www.law.cornell.edu/wex/in_loco_parentis.
5. Peace Amid & After Trauma, "Unaddressed Trauma: Ignoring Trauma Does Not Make It Go Away," accessed October 2, 2024, https://peaceaftertrauma.com/resources2/unaddressed-trauma/.
6. Beth Shaw, "When Trauma Gets Stuck in the Body," Psychology Today, October 23, 2019, https://www.

psychologytoday.com/us/blog/in-the-body/201910/when-trauma-gets-stuck-in-the-body.

7   Part 1, Title 9, Chapter 5.5, Sex Offenders, Code 293, "Of Crimes Against the Person Involving Sexual Assault, and Crimes against Public Decency and Good Morals," California Legislative Information, accessed October 2, 2024, https://leginfo.legislature.ca.gov/faces/codes_displaySection.xhtml?lawCode=PEN&sectionNum=293.

8   Elsie Ndibuagu Daluchi, "Childhood Trauma and Its Effects in Adulthood," *Global Journal of Applied, Management, and Social Sciences (GOJAMSS)* 21, January 2021, https://gojamss.net/journal/index.php/gojamss/article/view/656/634.

9   Darkness to Light, "The Issue of Child Sexual Abuse," Child Sexual Abuse Updates, accessed June 11, 2024, https://www.d2l.org/wp-content/uploads/2023/03/Child-Sexual-Abuse-Updates.pdf.

10 Indiana Center for the Prevention of Youth Abuse & Suicide, "Child Abuse Statistics," 2009-2022, https://www.indianaprevention.org/child-abuse-statistics.

11 Elizabeth L. Jeglic Ph.D., "It's Not Only Adults Who Perpetrate Child Sexual Abuse," Psychology Today, February 26, 2024, https://www.psychologytoday.com/us/blog/protecting-children-from-sexual-abuse/202402/is-it-only-adults-who-perpetrate-child-sexual.

ACKNOWLEDGEMENTS

First and foremost, I'd like to thank Jesus for blessing me with the opportunity to turn something dark into light. And for giving me hope for a very bright future and for placing amazing people in my path to accomplish that purpose.

I'd like to acknowledge my beautiful, loving children — Matt, Nick, and Sophia — for sticking by me in the darkness and for understanding my long hours at work, knowing that I was working toward a greater good.

Tom Brown, FBI: You are my rock, and I could never manage raising children and wearing so many hats without you and your support. Thank you for your undying love and devotion to our family.

I'd like to thank Wayne Gross, Alan Greenberg, and Brian Williams for giving me the opportunity to continue the good fight by advocating for survivors in a new arena.

To "Winston," the father I never had, the man who believed in me when I was "schleppin' hash" as a waitress — thank you for instilling in me hope, faith, and the promise of a great future. You saw something in me I hadn't seen in myself and gave me the opportunity to unlock my superpower. Thank you for enabling me to serve my community by working for decades to lock up predators while staying true to my authentic self. Your love, support, and encouragement carried me through my darkest hours. For that, I will be eternally grateful. I can't wait to be reunited in Heaven.

Thank you, Jemma Dunn, for answering all of my questions, teaching me the ropes, and showing me that civil attorneys work just as hard as criminal attorneys.

I can't thank Tom Masline enough for coming alongside me since I was 19 years old to guide, counsel, encourage, and help me navigate the transformation from waitress to lawyer.

Thank you to my law-enforcement friends and colleagues for embracing my "rough around the edges" style and encouraging me to be myself. I've come to know and love so many prosecutors and investigators that I'd have to write a book just to name them all, but you know who you are.

Matt Murphy, aka "MURPHY!", thank you for teaching me how to properly cross-examine expert witnesses and stay out of the weeds.

Robert Mestman, thank you for always answering your phone and citing case law for me in my time of need.

Jen Contini, Jennifer Duke, Hope Callahan, Rob Brown, and Sue Foley, thank you for helping me raise my children and for loving them as if they were your own.

Ava Bravo, I can't thank you enough for the nights in the SAU where you would sit with me to watch videos I couldn't bear to watch by myself, and for teaching me the value of standing up for your convictions, regardless of the consequences.

Thank you to John Beerling and Chris Petersen for being the best investigators Orange County has ever seen

ACKNOWLEDGEMENTS

and for keeping me sane during knock-down, drag-out court battles.

Thank you to Dr. Jodi Ward for teaching me about child sexual abuse victims' mindsets and the value of the expert witness.

Thank you to BACA (Bikers Against Child Abuse), Patricia Wenskunas, and Erin Merryl, who come alongside survivors of child abuse and fight to keep them safe, and most of all, for demonstrating that ordinary people can do extraordinary things to help victims thrive.

Thank you to all of my hooligan friends for loving me and celebrating my triumphs and failures. Kevin Chene, Kevin Smith, Frank Pennachio, Mike Procopio, Tracey Zimmerman, Vivien Hjort, Salberg, and Robin Sax, you are my village and have taught me that authentic relationships and laughter are what carry us through the darkest times.

Thank you to the judges who know and uphold the law, especially the Honorable Richard King, Gary Paer, Richard Neidorf, and retired Judges Gary Pohlson and Marty Engquist for being examples of how great judges administer justice.

Thank you, Patty and Howard Bolter, for providing me with my California family and treating me like your own.

Thank you to my beloved stepfather, Bob Talanian, for showing my mom what true love is and for being one of my greatest fans. You meant the world to our family, and we are forever grateful for you and Robyn Chojnowski for making our family truly complete. I can't wait to eat Sunday supper and watch the New England Patriots with you in Heaven.

Thank you to my dear Godmother, Sue Jacobs, for instilling in me a love of Jesus that has gotten me through the darkest times and for teaching me that the light shines brightest in the darkest places.

Maureen Kirby, your unwavering friendship for more than 50 years is more valuable than gold.

To my amazing brothers, Teddy and Tommy, thank you for always loving me, sticking up for me, and teaching me how to be scrappy.

Last but not least, I'd like to thank my mother, Stephanie, for teaching me to be a good person, to love others no matter how broken they are, and that when life pushes you down, you get back up and fight.

ABOUT GREENBERG GROSS

Greenberg Gross LLP, or GG for short, is a boutique trial law firm that represents clients in their most significant matters. With offices in California, Nevada, and New York, GG has helped clients across the country achieve extraordinary results in high-stakes cases.

Greenberg Gross LLP was founded with a single goal in mind: to provide the best possible service to clients involved in high-stakes litigation. Our team has evolved into a top-tier litigation firm known for representing survivors of sexual abuse, physical assault, and other serious personal injuries. Sexual abuse and serious personal injuries can result in trauma that can last decades. If you or a loved one were a victim, we are your dedicated, compassionate, empathetic advocate. We will stand by your side and fight for you, your future, and the justice and compensation you deserve so you can get closure. We take the time to get to know every client so we can tailor a solution that best fits his or her goals and needs.

Our two founding partners have been named among the top 100 lawyers in California. Others have been listed by national publications as "litigation stars," "best lawyers," "top women lawyers," "super lawyers," and "trailblazers." The firm is routinely listed as one of the country's "Best Law Firms" by U.S. News Media Group.

CONTACT

Website: FightForSurvivors.com
GGTrialLaw.com

LinkedIn: LinkedIn.com/Company/FightForSurvivors/

Instagram: Instagram.com/Fight4Survivors/

Facebook: Facebook.com/FightForSurvivors

YouTube: Youtube.com/@FightForSurvivors

TikTok: Tiktok.com/@FightForSurvivors

ABOUT THE AUTHOR

Heather Brown is a remarkable woman who has dedicated her life to seeking justice and empowering survivors of sexual abuse. With over 24 years of experience as a prosecutor in the Orange County District Attorney"s Office, Heather has relentlessly fought against evil, prosecuting hundreds of rapists and child molesters. Her unwavering commitment to protecting the vulnerable led her to work in the Sexual Assault Unit for over a decade, where she fearlessly advocated for victims.

Driven by a deep sense of justice, Heather transitioned to the Homicide Unit for five years, fearlessly prosecuting murderers and seeking closure for grieving families. Now, as a special counsel at Greenberg Gross LLP, within their dedicated practice group, Fight for Survivors, she continues her mission by litigating cases against schools, institutions, and churches that turn a blind eye to or have covered up child sexual abuse. Heather's work serves as a call to action, urging society to stand up against those who perpetrate and conceal these heinous crimes.

Heather also serves on the board of a nonprofit organization called Thriving in Freedom. This organization is committed to helping victims of human trafficking fund education and find meaningful employment. She also volunteers for a ministry that works toward helping victims of human trafficking escape from the clutches of sexual slave labor.

In addition to her advocacy work, Heather has been an adjunct professor at California State University, Fullerton, for the past 13 years, teaching a course called "Sex, Crime, and Culture." This allows her the opportunity to educate students about the complex intersections of these topics and to foster a deeper understanding of the issues surrounding sexual abuse and crime.

She has recently started a True Crime Podcast called Defeating the Darkness; True Crime Stories with Downtown Heather Brown, which profiles true crime stories and those in the community who work tirelessly to bring light to the darkness for victims of crime.

Heather's diverse experiences, both professionally and personally, have shaped her into a formidable advocate and compassionate individual who has become a trusted ally for victims and survivors. Her resilience and determination to make a difference extends beyond the courtroom as she continues to champion the rights of victims and survivors while educating others about the realities of sexual abuse and crime.

In addition to her professional achievements, Heather is a devoted wife and mother. Married for over 20 years to Tom, a retired FBI agent, she resides in Southern California with two of their three children. Their oldest son, Matthew, is a drone pilot serving in the United States Marine Corps, while their other son, Nicholas, is an exceptional athlete

ABOUT THE AUTHOR

and scholar who recently graduated high school and is attending Eastern Washington University on a football scholarship. Their daughter, Sophia, is an accomplished musician, showcasing her talent as a member of an award-winning school band, where she plays the baritone.

Outside of her professional and family life, Heather finds solace in various activities. She enjoys hiking, traveling, dancing, and engaging in weightlifting and Pilates workouts. Her true joy, however, lies in spending quality time with her loved ones and cultivating authentic and meaningful relationships. Heather cherishes the bonds she has formed within the law enforcement community and her circle of friends.

FIGHT FOR SURVIVORS
A DIVISION OF GREENBERG GROSS LLP

OVER $400 MILLION
IN VERDICTS AND SETTLEMENTS

ARE YOU OR SOMEONE YOU KNOW READY TO TAKE THE NEXT STEP TOWARDS JUSTICE AND HEALING?

CALL US TODAY
(833) 55-FIGHT

DEFEATING THE DARKNESS

TRUE CRIME PODCAST
WITH "DOWNTOWN"
HEATHER BROWN

Made in the USA
Middletown, DE
15 March 2025